JAPAN 2000

RUSSIA

NORTH
KOREA

SOUTH
KOREA

Korea Strait

EAST
CHINA
SEA

SEA OF JAPAN

HOKKAIDO

• Asahikaw

HOKKAIDO

• Sapporo

Hakodate •

AOMORI • Aomori

AKITA

Akita • • Morioka

IWATE

Kitakami River

Iwadeyama • • Toyoma
YAMAGATA   Rifu • MIYAGI
Yamagata • • Sendai
Natori
• Marumori
Niigata • *Agano River* Fukushima •

NIIGATA   TOCHIGI   FUKUSHIMA
ISHIKAWA   FUKUSHIMA

Shinano River   • Tōkamachi

TOYAMA   GUMMA   Utsunomiya
Toyama •   • Nagano   Maebashi •   Mito •
Kanazawa •   Karuizawa •   Matsuida •   *Tone River*
FUKUI   GIFU   NAGANO   SAITAMA   IBARAKI
Fukui •   *Kiso River*   Urawa •   Tsukuba •
Motosu •   *Tenryū River*   YAMANASHI
KYOTO   SHIGA   Gifu •   Kōfu • TOKYO   Chiba •
Kyoto •   Ōtsu •   AICHI   Yokohama •   CHIBA
OKAYAMA   HYŌGO   Tsu •   Nagoya   KANAGAWA
Okayama •   Kobe •   Osaka •   Shizuoka •
HIROSHIMA   OSAKA   Nara •   SHIZUOKA
Hiroshima •   Takamatsu •   NARA   MIE
KAGAWA   Wakayama •
Tokushima •   WAKAYAMA
TOKUSHIMA

HONSHŪ

TOTTORI
Yonago •
Matsue •   • Tottori

SHIMANE

YAMAGUCHI
Yamaguchi •

FUKUOKA
Kitakyūshū •
SAGA   Fukuoka •
Saga •   ŌITA
NAGASAKI   • Ōita
Nagasaki •   Kumamoto •   Soyō •
KUMAMOTO   Sakamoto •
Kuma
Yunomae •   KYŪSHŪ
KAGOSHIMA   MIYAZAKI
Kagoshima •   • Miyazaki

Matsuyama •   • Kōchi
EHIME   KŌCHI

SHIKOKU

PACIFIC OCEAN

JAPAN

↑
N

100 miles

OKINAWA
↙

JAPAN 2000

Architecture and Design
for the
Japanese Public

Edited by
John Zukowsky

Compiled by
Naomi R. Pollock, Tetsuyuki Hirano, and Tetsuro Hakamada

With essays by
John Heskett, Takuo Hirano, Tadanori Nagasawa,
Naomi R. Pollock, and Hiroyuki Suzuki

Prestel

Munich · New York

The Art Institute of Chicago
and The Japan Foundation

This book was published in conjunction with the exhibition "Japan 2000: Architecture and Design for the Japanese Public," coorganized by The Art Institute of Chicago and The Japan Foundation and shown in two parts, architecture and design, in the Art Institute's Kisho Kurokawa Gallery of Architecture from February 21 through May 3 and June 6 through September 7, 1998, respectively. The exhibitions were held alternately in the galleries of San Francisco International Airport that year as well. They subsequently traveled, in early 1999, to the Haus der Kulturen der Welt and the Internationales Design Zentrum, both in Berlin, through the support of Lufthansa German Airlines.

Contributions by all Japanese authors were translated by The Japan Foundation
Copyedited by Michele Schons, Munich
Copublished by The Art Institute of Chicago,
111 South Michigan Avenue, Chicago, Illinois, 60603-6110, USA
and by Prestel-Verlag

Front cover: Okayama West Police Station, Arata Isozaki & Associates, architects (Plates, no. 7)
Back cover: Midget II, Daihatsu (G-Mark 1996; Plates, no. 31)
Frontispiece: Map of Japan

The exhibition and this book were made possible by The Art Institute of Chicago's Architecture Exhibitions and Publications Fund, a challenge grant from the Graham Foundation for Advanced Studies in the Fine Arts, and the Architecture and Design Society of The Art Institute of Chicago. A grant from the Japan-United States Friendship Commission subsidized the publication of this catalogue. Additional support was also provided by Daihatsu Motor Co., Ltd., the Japanese Chamber of Commerce and Industry of Chicago, Mitsubishi Motors Corporation, and TOTO, Ltd. Japan Airlines supported the transportation of the exhibitions across the Pacific. This book is a publication of the Ernest R. Graham Study Center for Architectural Drawings at The Art Institute of Chicago.

Prestel books are available worldwide.

Please contact your nearest bookseller or write to either of the following addresses
for information concerning your local distributor:
Prestel-Verlag, Mandlstrasse 26, D-80802 Munich, Germany
Tel.: +49-89-38 17 090; Fax: +49-89-38 17 09 35
e-mail: prestel@compuserve.com
and 16 West 22nd Street, New York, NY 10010, USA
Tel.: (212) 627-8199; Fax: (212) 627-9866

Die Deutsche Bibliothek – CIP-Einheitsaufnahme

Japan 2000: architecture and design for the Japanese public / The Art Institute of Chicago and The Japan Foundation. Ed. by John Zukowsky. Comp. by Naomi R. Pollock... With essays by John Heskett.... – Munich; New York: Prestel, 1997

Designed by Heinz Ross, Munich

Map by Astrid Fischer, Munich
Color separations by Horlacher & Partner, Heilbronn
Printed on acid-free paper "LuxoMatt," 150 g/sm
Printed by Passavia Druckerei GmbH, Hutthurm near Passau
Bound by R. Oldenbourg GmbH, Kirchheim near Munich

Printed in Germany

ISBN 3-7913-1906-X (hardcover edition)
ISBN 0-86559-164-4 (softcover edition)

Contents

James N. Wood	7	Foreword
Shinichiro Asao	9	Foreword
John Zukowsky	11	Acknowledgments
John Zukowsky	15	Introduction

19 Architecture

Hiroyuki Suzuki	21	The Historical Background of Postwar Public Architecture in Japan
Naomi R. Pollock	31	Designing for the Japanese Public
Naomi R. Pollock	49	Plates

81 Design

John Heskett	83	The Growth of Industrial Design in Japan
Takuo Hirano	95	The History of Japanese Design: A Personal View
Tadanori Nagasawa	101	The Cultural Engineering of Traditional Local Industry
Tetsuyuki Hirano and Tetsuro Hakamada	113	Plates

147	Biographical Glossary
155	Contributors
157	Index
158	Photography Credits

Foreword

The Art Institute of Chicago has long had ties with Japan. Owing to the generosity of Clarence and Kate Buckingham, collectors of Japanese art who were patrons of this museum beginning in 1925, the Art Institute was able to acquire an impressive collection of Asian art, which includes major examples of all phases of the Japanese wood-block print that were in Clarence Buckingham's own collection. More recently, in 1992, our Asian collections were reinstalled in greatly expanded galleries. This major reinstallation includes a gallery for Japanese screens designed by architect Tadao Ando – his first American space. But, when this was opened, Chicago was no stranger to the work of Japan's famous architects.

During the decade of economic growth in the 1980s, Japanese architects executed buildings in Chicago as in other cities throughout Europe and America. The first of these in Chicago were built for the E. F. Hauserman furniture company, whose showroom in the Merchandise Mart was designed by Arata Isozaki in 1982. This was the architect's first completed work in the United States, preceding the completion of his well-known Museum of Contemporary Art in Los Angeles by several years. Although the Hauserman showroom no longer exists, Chicago's visitors and residents alike can experience local examples by Japanese architects by viewing the American Medical Association Building by Kenzo Tange or the Sporting Club, in the Illinois Center, by Kisho Kurokawa, both examples constructed in 1988-90.

The city's fascination with Japanese architecture will doubtless continue now that Tadao Ando has completed a private home in Lincoln Park. In recent years, our own Department of Architecture acquired the drawings and models for a number of these Chicago structures and spaces, as well as additional drawings by Tadao Ando, Kisho Kurokawa, and Kenzo Tange. Even more than the work of Japan's architects, Japanese design has been a part of everyday life in Chicago for the last several decades.

With this fortified American connection to Japan's design environment, it is natural that our museum's Department of Architecture should work with the very capable staff of The Japan Foundation to organize two exhibitions of the latest work by Japanese architects and designers under the title "Japan 2000." The work has, at its core, a basis in Japanese government policies on design, be they national, regional, or local. It is especially fitting that an art museum such as ours examine the role of government in the design arts at a time when our own federal and state agencies that support art, architecture, and culture have been struggling to survive and attempting to justify their expenditure within our society.

Both exhibitions have been created under the leadership of John Zukowsky, our Curator of Architecture, who worked with guest curators, architect Naomi R. Pollock and industrial designer Tetsuyuki Hirano, among others, to realize both exhibitions and the present accompanying volume for an American audience. We appreciate all their work on this project as well as the support of corporate sponsors who have endorsed their efforts to examine the role of architecture and design within Japanese society today.

James N. Wood
Director and President
The Art Institute of Chicago

Foreword

The Japan Foundation is pleased to announce the opening of two ambitious exhibitions at The Art Institute of Chicago under the general title "Japan 2000," introducing aspects of contemporary Japanese architecture and design.

Just over a century ago, in 1893, the World's Columbian Exposition opened in Chicago commemorating the 400th anniversary of Columbus's arrival on the North American continent. At that fair, the Japanese government set up a pavilion modeled after the eleventh-century temple, Byodo-in, commonly known as the "Phoenix Hall," landscaped in the style of a traditional Japanese garden, and placed on display a wide array of traditional works of art and craftsmanship. The exotic content and atmosphere of the pavilion is said to have been an extremely popular attraction at the exposition. It was, in fact, the first time that Frank Lloyd Wright, whose architectural activities were then based in Chicago, came into contact with Japanese architecture.

Wright went on to establish close ties with Japan, designing a number of buildings later built there, including the well-known Imperial Hotel. He became an enthusiastic collector and procurer of Ukiyo-e wood-block prints, the results of which are on exhibition at The Art Institute of Chicago. The city was thus one of the pivotal points of the "Japonisme" movement in the United States.

To have this opportunity of introducing Japanese architecture and design to this great city – this time on the eve of a new millennium – is not only a great honor, but it strikes one also as being an occasion of great historical significance. Over the more than one hundred years that have passed since 1893, society and life in Japan have been profoundly influenced by the United States and Europe, and people's values and attitudes have changed tremendously. In the architectural works and the mass-market industrial design products exhibited here, one will no longer find much trace of anything that could be defined as "uniquely Japanese." More remarkable, in fact, is their expression of a shared spirit and sense of priorities that transcends national boundaries. The pieces included in these exhibitions are a reflection of the sensibilities and life-styles of contemporary Japanese. Indeed, I believe they can be seen as a portrait in miniature of the political, economic, cultural, and social environment of Japan today.

The works in the architecture exhibition focus on public buildings. This is a genre that is continually concerned with the problem of "for whom" architecture is built, and which labors under many and diverse restraints. The works presented here display the variety in content and scale that typifies a time of rapidly diversifying popular values. The fascination of this exhibition will be to see how each architect manages to realize his or her own concepts and ideas, while incorporating considerations of the different groups of people involved in the project.

The design exhibition focuses, in part, on industrial designs that have won the "G-Mark" insignia bestowed by the Ministry of International Trade and Industry under its program for promoting high-quality design products. Through G-Mark awarded products, the development of Japanese industrial design is traced from the end of World War II to contemporary design based on fresh, up-to-date sensibilities.

We would like to take this opportunity to express our gratitude to the owners, architects, and designers who have generously made available works in their possession for display in this exhibition. We would also like to express our special thanks to The Art Institute of Chicago, the coorganizer of these exhibitions, and to guest curator Naomi R. Pollock, as well as to the many other persons involved in both Japan and the United States without whose devoted efforts the exhibitions would not have been possible.

Shinichiro Asao
President
The Japan Foundation

ACKNOWLEDGMENTS

While on a trip to Japan in 1995, I had the opportunity to meet with Naomi R. Pollock, an American architect and writer on architecture, who lives in Tokyo, and I thought that she would be a most appropriate person to curate an exhibition of contemporary Japanese architecture. That visit also took me to a variety of architects' offices to see their latest work and, over the next few months, plans for the architecture exhibition began to take shape, in part, with the advice of architect Kisho Kurokawa, as well as the diligent work of Naomi R. Pollock. Those who advised her deserve our thanks, and include: Arata Isozaki, Fumihiko Maki, Kengo Kuma, Riichi Miyake, Kinya Maruyama, Shinichi Okada, Riken Yamamoto, Hiroshi Hara, Hideto Horike, Shozo Baba, Hiroyuki Suzuki, Yoshiteru Kaneko, Toyo Ito, Mamoru Adachi, Takashi Yokoi, Akira Miyata, Hajime Yatsuka, Yoshio Taniguchi, and Yoko Kinoshita.

But what about design? This was to be an integral part of the project, but neither of us were specialists in contemporary Japanese design. Fortunately, one of the board members of our Architecture and Design Society, Hiroshi Ariyama, who works for Hirano Design in Chicago, introduced us to Tetsuyuki Hirano in Tokyo. He was very generous in devoting himself and his staff's time to help create the design component of this project. Tetsuro Hakamada, a manager in his company, who was assisted by Jin Kuse, Senior Designer, and Mondo Kasano, Assistant Designer, worked with an advisory committee to curate the design portion of this volume. The committee members include: Shiro Aoki, General Manager, Japan Industrial Design Promotion Organization; Kazuo Kawasaki, Professor, Nagoya City University School of Design and Architecture; Kozo Sato, President, Kozo Design Studio; Tadanori Nagasawa, MARCA Design Consultant/Cultural Engineer; Naomi R. Pollock; and Takao Shimizu, Director, Design Policy Office Industrial Policy Bureau, MITI (Ministry of International Trade and Industry).

With this fine team working on the architecture and design exhibitions, we developed the theme of government in relation to the design arts, in part, to serve as a contrast to the decentralized and free-market approach to architecture and design as practiced in the United States. With this theme in mind, we approached

The Japan Foundation to support our efforts, and they generously agreed to share the responsibilities with us in organizing this venture. We are grateful to their staff for helping to realize this project: Takakuni Inoue, former Director of the Arts Department, Exhibition Division, and the current Director, Hayato Ogo; Assistant Director Mana Takatori, and her colleagues, Masanobu Ito and Naomi Koyama, all in Tokyo; and the staff then at the New York office, particularly Natsuo Amemiya, Director General, and Satoshi Yura, Assistant Director. Under the auspices of The Japan Foundation, Hiroshi Watanabe provided us with English translations of the architectural texts. Because the Japanese Consulate in Chicago provided much needed advice, their staff deserve our gratitude as well: Mitsuyoshi Nishimura, the former Consul General as well as the current Consul General, Tomoyuki Abe; and the members of the Japan Information Center, Joji Miyamori, Director; Chikako Banno, Vice Consul; and Shinji Yamada, Special Assistant.

As the exhibition was assembled over three years, we received a grant from the Japan-United States Friendship Commission to help publish this catalogue. Eric J. Gangloff, their Executive Director, and Margaret P. Mihori, Assistant Executive Director, were very supportive of our efforts. Additional financial support was received from Daihatsu Motor Co., Ltd., the Japanese Chamber of Commerce and Industry of Chicago, Mitsubishi Motors Corporation, and TOTO, Ltd. With this firm fiscal and intellectual basis for the project, numerous people in Japan and the United States assisted us to make it a reality. Elsa Cameron, Director, John Hill, Curator of the Aviation Library, and Blake Summers, all from the Bureau of Fine Arts and Exhibitions at San Francisco International Airport, were enthusiastic about these exhibitions coming to their galleries within the terminal spaces. Hans Georg Knopp, Director of the Haus der Kulturen der Welt, and Angela Schönberger, Director of the Internationales Design Zentrum, shared an equal amount of enthusiasm for holding these exhibitions in Berlin, with the support of the Chicago office of Lufthansa German Airlines. Staff members of architectural and design offices in Tokyo helped provide information for the exhibition and they deserve our thanks as well: Akiko Sato, Secretary to Kisho Kurokawa; Kazunori Hiruta of Naito Architect & Associates; Akiko Kanie of Itsuko Hasegawa Atelier; Yoshiko Amiya of Arata Isozaki & Associates; Koichiro Tokimori of Kazuyo Sejima & Associates; Mayumi Sakuramoto of Toyo Ito & Associates, Architects; Yuko Kitamura of Riken Yamamoto & Field Shop; and Gary Kamemoto of Maki and Associates. Two other individuals in Chicago who assisted our efforts are Stanley Tigerman and Victor Margolin, who provided advice on the architecture and design exhibits, respectively. We especially would like to extend our heartfelt thanks to the authors. They have contributed rare knowledge to this volume and to our understanding of architecture and design in Japanese society today.

Finally, we wish to thank a number of Art Institute employees for their work on this project. First and foremost among them are Karin Victoria, Director of Government Relations, who was assisted by Jennifer Harris, Greg Cameron, former Director of Corporate and Foundation Relations, and Meredith Miller-Hayes, Associate Director. Their help was essential to secure sufficient funding for this project and Karin, in particular, was integral to the development of the relationship between the Art Institute and the Japan Foundation. Our departmental secretary, Linda Adelman, typed the plate entries, labels, and other relevant materials published here. Annie Morse and Annabelle Clarke of the Department of Imaging and Technical Services assisted in providing photographs.

Advice and assistance regarding the financial operations for the exhibition were provided by Robert E. Mars, Executive Vice President of Administrative Affairs; Calvert W. Audrain, Assistant Vice President of Administrative Affairs – Operations; and Dorothy M. Schroeder, Assistant Director of Exhibitions and Budget. Executive Director of Registration, Mary Solt, with the assistance of Darrell Green, Associate Registrar for Loans and Exhibitions, ensured that the pieces on loan were appropriately recorded, and they organized the complex shipping arrangements for the works on display. The architectural drawings were expertly framed by Caesar Citraro. Reynold V. Bailey, Manager of Art Handling, and his staff carefully installed the objects, working closely with William Caddick and Ronald Pushka, Director and Assistant Director, respectively, of the Physical Plant, and his staff, particularly William Hey. Ann Wassmann, Associate Director of Graphic Design in the Department of Graphic Design and Communications, thoughtfully prepared the graphics for both exhibition installations in collaboration with Hiroshi Ariyama, who designed the exhibitions, and Gary Heitz, of Chicago Scenic Design, who constructed them. Finally, the Public Affairs Department, under Executive Director Eileen Harakal and with the assistance of John Hindman, promoted the exhibition to a wide audience before and after the opening to the public.

John Zukowsky
Curator of Architecture
The Art Institute of Chicago

It is a well-known fact that Japanese architecture and design acquired international prominence in the boom decade of the 1980s. Japanese products, from automobiles to electronic equipment, were sold in record numbers the world over. The names Honda, Toyota, Nissan, Sony, and Panasonic, among others, became synonymous with high-quality products. Prominent Japanese architects, such as Tadao Ando, Arata Isozaki, Toyo Ito, Kisho Kurokawa, Fumihiko Maki, and Kenzo Tange, designed buildings erected in Europe and the United States, from Berlin and Paris to Chicago, Los Angeles, and San Francisco, from the mid-1980s through the early 1990s. Japanese architects won, and continue to win, international acclaim through prestigious architectural awards, such as the Pritzker Prize for Architecture presented to Kenzo Tange (1987), Fumihiko Maki (1993), and Tadao Ando (1995). Nevertheless, one views and visits their works, buys and uses those brand-name products outside the context of their creation. Are the famous buildings illustrated in the latest Western architectural magazines representative of the architecture found in contemporary Japan? What products are available there that are not marketed in the West, and why?

Now that the boom of the 1980s (or, as it is called in Japan, the era of the "bubble" economy) has come to an end and Japan has entered a period of limited growth, along with much of the rest of the world, what is the country's designed and built environment like? This book and the exhibition it accompanies attempt to present the design era of the post-boom 1990s to a Western audience for the first time. More importantly, the authors have tried to place these new buildings and products within the wider context of government's role in relation to architecture and design in Japan.

During my visits to Japan over the past few years of working on this project, several points have struck me as important in understanding the context from which the works of the 1990s have emerged. Noteworthy and significant are the Japanese traditions of politeness, formality, punctuality, and cleanliness, all of which can be explained only as their way of controlling the high density and the potential chaos of their spatially restrictive surroundings. The visual environment – from the diverse, con-

Fig. 1
Shibuya district, Tokyo

15

Fig. 2
High-rise buildings under construction near the Port of Tokyo, 1995 (Kenzo Tange's Fuji TV headquarters are on the left)

centrated cityscapes to the ever-present profusion of graphics, to the numerous large-scale televisions and other electronic gadgets on display – reflects this pandemonium (Fig. 1). To paraphrase the words of one Japanese designer, the Japanese people are adept at blocking out their surroundings. A further visual characteristic concerns the extremes of scale. One can see clusters of high-rise buildings, randomly intermingled with their low-rise cousins, as well as new high-rise structures sprouting from reclaimed land (Fig. 2) – all of which is part of the urban jumble that sprawls for miles. The high concentration of some of these urban and suburban regions is staggering. For instance, the Kanto Plain that surrounds Tokyo boasts an estimated population of some 70 million, whereas the Kansai region around Kobe and Osaka claims some 30 million residents. Needless to say, traffic jams abound, not only in the congested urban areas, but also on the ubiquitous and often enormous overhead, multi-lane highways that traverse the country. Even the road leading to the multi-level terminal of the new Kansai International Airport takes the form of an elevated highway (Fig. 3). The cars that roll along these gigantic thoroughfares are surprisingly homogeneous in appearance – gray, taupe, white, or black – much like the muted tones of the business suits worn by white-collar workers, the so-called "salarymen," in Japanese companies. It seems that vibrant colors, such as hazard or industrial yellow, are reserved only for trucks and industrial equipment. Even in browsing through the color plate section of this volume, one cannot help but notice the restrained, business-like homogeneity of the buildings and the designed objects.

This sprawl, this controlled jumble within a contained environment, provides the background for those set-pieces designed

Fig. 3
Service road at the Kansai International Airport, Tokyo, 1994

Fig. 4
Nikken Sekkei, architects.
Tokorozawa Aviation Museum,
Tokorozawa 1993

by Japan's finest architects, that we see published in architectural monographs and magazines. Seen at first hand, many of these jewels outshine, rather than blend into, their environments – and it is easy to see why. They are often beautifully detailed, with construction budgets of up to $700 to $800 per square foot for some cultural and institutional facilities – about three to four times the cost of such a building in the United States.

When one visits Japan one marvels not so much at the corporate headquarters or the spectacular high-rises, but at the wealth of small government-funded buildings and like constructions throughout the country, from concert halls and health-care facilities to police stations and museums of all kinds (Fig. 4). Many of these are financed by Japan's "prefectures," the equivalent of American states. Government's role as an architectural patron in Japan has become even more apparent in the recession-plagued 1990s, in which commercial development has generally come to a halt. This parallels governmental support of the design arts, most notably since the 1950s, with the G-Mark awards program for good design instituted by the Ministry of International Trade and Industry to promote a positive image for design throughout Japan.

It is, therefore, appropriate that we investigate what is at the core of Japan's design arts – the government, as patron and endorser. In so doing, we shall examine some of the latest ideas in the fields of Japanese architecture and design within the context of Japanese society as it prepares to enter into the next millennium. The authors describe the historical background to these contemporary developments, and portfolios of color plates and halftones provide the reader with an extensive overview of the latest trends in architecture and design in Japan.

ARCHITECTURE

Hiroyuki Suzuki — The Historical Background of Postwar Public Architecture in Japan

I

It was in July 1956 that the Economic Planning Agency declared in its *White Paper on the Economy* that "the postwar period is over." The agency made that memorable statement over a decade after the end of World War II, because living standards had recovered to prewar levels as a result of economic reconstruction, rising exports, and abundant harvests. Today, we look back on this fifty-year period not because we feel a need to re-examine the changes in our material well-being during that time, but, because with the passing of fifty years the postwar period is truly about to become history.

Even before fifty years had elapsed, modern architecture had won acceptance in Japan, and diverse modernist experiments had been carried out. The first architectural design competition held after the war was in 1948 for the World Peace Memorial Cathedral in Hiroshima (Fig. 1), followed soon thereafter by the competition for the Hiroshima Peace Center (Fig. 2). In each case, the result was a superb work of architecture that will long be admired. The architects of the two buildings, Togo Murano and Kenzo Tange, went on to become the two leading architects in postwar Japan.

The history of Japanese postwar architecture begins indisputably with these two works. However, in recent years divergent views have been voiced concerning the place in history of architecture from the 1950s, many examples of which still survive. The immediate cause of the debate is the threat of demolition, which buildings constructed in the period of redevelopment face. There are some who dispute the importance of modernist works, while favoring the preservation of buildings in other styles, such as works of revivalist architecture. However, there is no logical basis for such attitudes, and reactionary and irrational arguments of this kind will no doubt be repudiated.

We need to recognize that architectural works, including works of functionalist design, are important not only as expressions of the spirit of the age, that is, as works of art, but also as objects that bear witness to the age. One of the pleasures of studying and assessing architecture is to distinguish between great and mediocre works, and to judge this or that masterpiece worthy of

Fig. 1
Togo Murano, architect.
World Peace Memorial Cathedral,
Hiroshima, 1955

being designated a "national treasure" or an "important cultural asset." However, it is dangerous to use such evaluations as criteria for the preservation of buildings. With works of the recent past, for example, those evaluations may be nothing more than arbitrary expressions of personal taste. In evaluating a work of architecture and in passing our judgment on to the next generation, we must objectively consider the spirit of the age embodied in the work.

Architecture that is fifty years old possesses a historical character, which carries implications for both modern architecture and modern history. The question is: "Has the postwar period in Japan been put into a historical perspective?" I am of the opinion that we do not yet have a shared historical viewpoint from which to consider the postwar period, or rather that our discussion of the subject has, as yet, been inadequate. The same can be said with respect to architecture of that period.

II

Let us now consider the contrasting careers of Tange and Murano. As I have stated, the two architects began their careers after the war with projects in Hiroshima. Tange designed while teaching at the University of Tokyo, and Murano ran his own office in Osaka. Tange designed mainly for central and local government, while Murano designed for the private sector.

Since Tokyo is the capital of Japan, government agencies are concentrated there; by contrast, Osaka has traditionally been a city of commerce. In their different ways these cities affect the nature of an architect's approach. It is only natural that Tange,

Fig. 2
Kenzo Tange, architect.
Peace Center, Hiroshima, 1949-55

1   Kenzo Tange, *Sengo kenchiku no kita michi yuku michi* (The Road Traveled and the Road Ahead of Postwar Architecture) (Tokyo, 1995), p. 186.

based in Tokyo, be involved in government-related work and Murano, based in Osaka, be active in the private sector.

Public architecture in postwar Japan was unlike public architecture before the war. There are two reasons for this. First, postwar Japan faced the task of reconstructing cities that had been damaged in the war, and second, the nature of local government had changed in a fundamental way.

Looking back on the period, Tange writes:

> Soon after the end of the war, the War-Damage Reconstruction Board, which later evolved into the Ministry of Construction, began to develop plans all over the country in its efforts to formulate a reconstruction policy for cities damaged in the war. However, there were no experts in the field as yet, and I was asked to assemble a team of young people doing research in the field of architecture. I had just become an assistant professor at the University of Tokyo upon finishing graduate school there. I had always wanted to do such work. Wishing to be assigned Hiroshima, where I had spent my high-school days, I, together with people in my research group such as Takashi Asada and Sachio Otani, announced our readiness to undertake city planning for the purpose of reconstructing Hiroshima. In the end I was put in charge of the effort. . . . I do not remember precisely how many such teams were at work, but there were quite a few.[1]

The city plans developed for the reconstruction were public plans, and the buildings created on the basis of those plans were public buildings.

Meanwhile, local government in Japan had undergone a fundamental change and this enabled a new architecture to develop. Before the war, prefectural governors had been appointed by the Ministry of the Interior, a central government agency. However, in 1947, a new Constitution came into effect and at the same time a new Local Government Law was enacted. It was on the basis of that law that prefectural governors and mayors of municipalities came to be chosen directly by the people through election. The Ministry of the Interior, which had exercised control over localities until that time, was abolished on February 27 of that year. Since each prefecture and municipality now chose its own head, the construction of local government buildings, which served as symbols of local autonomy, became an important part of postwar urban reconstruction.

Tange began his architectural career after the war, and the majority of his architectural works erected in the postwar period consisted of public buildings of that kind, such as the Hiroshima Reconstruction City Plan of 1946-47, the Hiroshima Peace Center of 1949-55 (Fig. 2), the Tokyo Metropolitan Government Building of 1952-57, the Kagawa Prefectural Government Building of 1955-58 (Fig. 3), and Kurashiki City Hall of 1958-60. His only non-public building from that time was his own residence, designed in 1953.

Fig. 3
Kenzo Tange, architect.
Kagawa Prefectural Government
Building, Takamatsu, 1955-58

In 1961, he presented the "Tokyo Plan 1960," which, in expressing his vision of the city, constituted a further development of his new imagery in the arena of public architecture.

In the same period, Murano was working in Osaka, designing hotels, department stores, theaters (Fig. 4), and company housing. It was only in the late 1950s that he tried his hand at anything that could be described as public architecture. The results were Yonago City Public Hall in 1958 and Yokohama City Hall in 1960. In fact, by the end of the 1950s, many architects were active

Fig. 4
Togo Murano, architect.
New Kabuki Theater, Osaka, 1958

24   *Hiroyuki Suzuki*

in the field of public architecture. Some well-known architects gained experience in public architecture, such as Seiichi Shirai, who designed the Matsuida Town Office and Akinomiya Village Office, and Takeo Sato, who designed Asahikawa City Hall. Kunio Maekawa, who had made strenuous efforts before the war to win acceptance of modern architecture in Japan, was engaged in the design of many public buildings at this time.

Postwar public architecture was on the cutting edge, disseminating democratic ideals and the spirit of modernity throughout Japan. There was an underlying belief in universal space, that embodiment of the modern spirit, in the design of public buildings. Public architecture became synonymous with modern architecture.

III

The modern spirit in prewar Japan was compounded of a belief in the absolute righteousness of the self and a desire to enlighten and civilize the external world. Even intellectuals belonging to the so-called "war generation" tended to see themselves as victims of the system that had produced the war, rather than as victimizers. It was the architects belonging to this generation, including Tange, who gave architectural expression to local autonomy in the postwar period. Modern public architecture flourished in the fertile soil of postwar Japan, and at the center of it all was Kenzo Tange.

Doubts about modern architecture surfaced in Japan in the late 1960s. Arata Isozaki, a disciple of Tange who belongs to the next generation, recalls that things came to a head in 1968, the year of student rebellion. No hard evidence has ever been presented to substantiate the claim that the university upheavals had an effect on Japanese architecture. Nevertheless, many people feel that they had a decisive influence on the intellectual – or anti-intellectual – climate of postwar Japan.

From March to June 1968, university students protested publicly around the world as if in sympathetic response to the demonstrations by students and workers in Paris. The student protests at the University of California at Berkeley are well known. Those in Japan were referred to as the "Zenkyōtō Movement," because an organization called "Zengaku Kyōtō Kaigi" (All-Campus Joint Struggle Committee), or "Zenkyōtō" for short, was the guiding force. The movement climaxed in Japan at Nihon University and the University of Tokyo, and, at the latter, riot police were dispatched in January 1969 to reopen Yasuda Auditorium (Fig. 5), which had been taken over by students. Entrance examinations were canceled at the University of Tokyo that year.

Fig. 5 Yoshikazu Uchida, architect. Yasuda Auditorium, University of Tokyo

This description of the mere externals of the movement fails to convey its significance, and even today no true consensus has been reached on the historical significance of the Zenkyōtō Movement. Nevertheless, the generation that was involved in this movement is still referred to as the "Zenkyōtō generation" and continues to hold its own views. What were the issues raised by the movement? The introduction to *Toride no ueni warerano sekai o* ([Seeking] Our World Above the Fortress), written by Yoshitaka Yamamoto, then chairman of the Zenkyōtō chapter at the University of Tokyo, sheds light on the spiritual climate of the time:

> The situation in which one finds oneself is also inside oneself. That which is to be censured can first be discovered inside the self, and the logic of indictment is condensed above all inside the self. Ideology cannot act upon the world if one engages in the thought outside the world. Thinking that closely adheres to a situation cuts through to the heart of the situation and attains universality, and that becomes possible with the denial and reform of the thinking object.[2]

Some may find Yamamoto's writing obscure, but his stance is clear enough and typical of the time. He declares that criticism of the world must begin with criticism of the self. To deny the self is first to recognize one's own guilt and wrongdoing. Only when one has achieved that recognition can one act upon the external world. Zenkyōtō called on people to recognize their own culpability as victimizers and to act on the basis of that recognition.

The slogan of the May Revolution in Paris – "It is forbidden to forbid" – was also a rejection of authority's right to prohibit unilaterally. In that sense, the movement was a struggle, not to usurp

2 Yoshitaka Yamamoto, *Toride no ueni warerano sekai o* ([Seeking] Our World Above the Fortress) (Tokyo, 1969).

Fig. 6
War Museum, Cambodia

authority, but to reject it. The movement was resolved not to become itself a claimant to authority. In Japan this stance was expressed as "self-denial." The self that was being denied was the modern intellect.

Thus, the university upheavals were essentially a cultural, not a political, struggle. They have that in common with the Cultural Revolution in China of 1966-76 and even with the mass executions in Cambodia by the Khmer Rouge under Pol Pot in the second half of the 1970s (Fig. 6). To call the policies of the Khmer Rouge a cultural movement may be objectionable, but Pol Pot was intent on cleansing Cambodia of what he saw as being modern, Western pollution.

Of what, then, was the modern spirit so guilty that it invited criticism from these movements?

IV

What the modern spirit had brought to pass was universality. The spaces created by Ludwig Mies van der Rohe are some of the finest expressions thereof, yet such spaces have undoubtedly also made our world uniform and characterless. However, universal spaces are so much a part of our modern character that to criticize them is to call our very being into question. We have, nevertheless, no choice but to confront the problem posed by such spaces: to us, they have robbed us of *place*. This is a fact that everyone will surely acknowledge.

In the movements I have cited, people rebelled against the elimination of individuality in the name of universality. In architecture, anything that was not universal was rejected. Individuality in architecture can be expressed in two ways: through ornament, which is contrary to the purity of architecture, and through place, which endows a building with presence. In the midst of Western modernization, both Pol Pot and Mao Zedong tried to recapture the place, or country, in which they were born and raised, and whose future they intended to determine. They undoubtedly realized the hopelessness of such a struggle at a time when globalization was becoming a reality.

It might have been supposed that restoring ornament or place to architecture was equally hopeless. After all, postwar public architecture had imposed a common vocabulary on architecture in Japan. The result had been the loss of identity by local cities and the emergence of an architectural expression that no longer depended on the character of place. Restoring what had been deficient in public architecture in the immediate postwar period, and endowing architecture with a new character of place, ought to have been a daunting task. However, architects chose to rein-

Fig. 7
Arata Isozaki, architect.
Tsukuba Center Building,
Tsukuba, 1978-83

terpret the historical context, giving birth to postmodernism. By using a formal vocabulary infused with meaning (i.e., historical motifs), architects succeeded, at a stroke, in forcing people to reconsider the universality implicit in modernism. Those active in other cultural spheres, astonished at this achievement, began, albeit belatedly, to employ the word "postmodern" as well. Architecture thus assumed ideological leadership in the arts.

After the advent of postmodernism, public buildings again played a central role in architecture. In contrast to the period of postwar reconstruction, public architecture after the 1970s focused on cultural facilities, such as museums and concert halls, not on local government buildings. The mainstream of public architecture no longer took the form of modernist buildings, imbued with the spirit of democracy, but of architecture that was postmodern in expression and diverse in design. The spotlight was now on Tange's disciples who had become the standard-bearers of the new style, Isozaki and Kisho Kurokawa. They have designed many public buildings but the best known are probably Isozaki's Tsukuba Center Building (Figs. 7, 8) and Kurokawa's National Museum of Ethnology (Fig. 9). In the Tsukuba Center Building, Isozaki intermittently employed Western architectural motifs, and in the National Museum of Ethnology, Kurokawa introduced into the courtyard an abstract composition that he called "a ruin for the future" (Fig. 10). Kurokawa made frequent use of Japanese motifs, which appeared in subsequent works, such as the National Bunraku Theater in Osaka.

Fig. 8   Arata Isozaki, architect.
Tsukuba Center Building, Tsukuba,
1978-83

Fig. 9
Kisho Kurokawa, architect.
National Museum of Ethnology,
Osaka, 1977

In every period, public architecture seems to embody most clearly the spirit of architectural expression of the time, and to that extent it reveals the spirit of the time. An examination of public architecture can give us an understanding of the architectural spirit of the time, but that may be because a concept of "public character" that transcends time does not exist in the architecture of Japan.

Fig. 10
Kisho Kurokawa, architect.
Central court of the National
Museum of Ethnology,
Osaka, 1977

In the 1990s, government became a leading patron of architecture in Japan. In the 1980s, a period of speculative excess referred to now as the "bubble" economy, it was commercial clients and their flashy commissions that had led the way. After the bursting of this bubble, public agencies helped to pick up the slack by hiring independent architects to design everything from police boxes and public toilets to sports arenas and regional art centers. Government entities have even sought architects for urban planning and civil engineering projects well beyond the usual scope of the architect's drawing board. And virtually every one of Japan's forty-seven prefectures has joined in the quest to augment its public facilities. With many of these projects coming to fruition as the twentieth century draws to a close, it seems appropriate to begin evaluating this body of work.

On one level, all buildings, regardless of who pays for them, are public. Even a private house has a public face. But unlike privately financed projects, buildings erected with public funds carry a greater obligation to respond to the needs of citizens as a whole if for no other reason than because it is the taxpayer who ultimately foots the bill. To fulfill this obligation, architects in Japan have adopted a wide variety of strategies. Some have attempted to create a sense of place. Others have tried to carve out well-defined spaces that people can imbue with meaning of their own. Still others have questioned and reconfigured programmatic types in an attempt to design buildings better tailored to their public audience. Granted, the results have not always been worthy of acclaim. In some instances, a seemingly unlimited budget and a free hand in design have allowed the architect to pursue an agenda that ignored the public's interests. In other cases, new public facilities have been criticized for their lack of planning and management after construction had been completed. But many projects have avoided these pitfalls. Among them are the seventeen examples presented in this volume, which should withstand the test of time and prove to have been public money well spent.

Recently, publicly funded projects in Japan have been undertaken by every level of government – from national and prefectural agencies down to cities, towns, and the smallest villages.

Fig. 1
Naoko Hirakura Associates, architects.
Rose Koban, police box (detail),
Tokyo, 1993

While this variety in clientele has fostered diversity, there are limits to its scope. Japan's forty-seven prefectures enjoy a modicum of autonomy, but they are far less independent of the national government than their U.S. counterparts, the fifty states. Most importantly, virtually all of Japan's public projects depend, at least in part, on the national government for financing. Frequently that assistance is accompanied by a certain amount of control over the end product.

Plans for public housing, for example, must fulfill the Public Housing Law's strict requirements in order to qualify for subsidies from the national government. And with financial support covering as much as 50 percent of the total cost, few local governments can afford not to comply. While lawmakers established much-needed construction standards after World War II, the law no longer guarantees comfortable living quarters. "The reason for this lies in the minimized dimensions and inflexible floor plans prescribed by strict planning requirements," explains architect Arata Isozaki.

Many public projects are directly under the aegis of national government ministries, which may have their own design agendas. In addition to the Ministry of Construction, which maintains offices throughout the country, numerous other ministries and agencies have in-house architecture departments. The Ministry of Posts and Telecommunications (formerly the Communications Ministry), for example, has a long history of pioneering new standards in public design dating back to the 1920s and 1930s, when it built a series of Secessionist and International Style facilities. "The Communications Ministry took pride in the image of speed and efficiency created throughout the nation . . . by its Architectural Department. Post Offices were the most numerous and representative building category, though other work turned out by the department included telephone and telegraph facilities, electrical and marine experimental stations, aerodromes, and lighthouses," explains architectural historian David Stewart.[1]

While government architects today continue to design buildings, many are turning their attention to administrative tasks. Of the work by outsiders, large architectural firms and construction companies continue to secure the greatest share of public commissions, but an increasingly wide circle of independent architects have also benefited – young and old, Tokyo-based and local, and even a few foreign designers. "While the total budget for public buildings has remained largely unchanged since the 1980s, in the past ten years local governments have increasingly started to make buildings of character," says Akira Miyata, Executive Director of the Public Buildings Association, which

1 David B. Stewart, *The Making of Modern Japanese Architecture* (New York, 1987), p. 13.
2 Hiroyuki Suzuki and Reyner Banham, *Contemporary Architecture of Japan, 1958-1984* (New York, 1985), p. 62.

researches the construction of public buildings. "Local governments want special buildings, so increasingly they are selecting atelier-type firms instead of big companies."

While recent changes in Japan's public buildings have been dramatic, this segment of design has evolved continuously over the post-World War II period as the result of a host of economic, social, and cultural factors. Immediately following World War II, Japan pressed to rebuild as quickly, safely, and cheaply as possible. In-house government design departments and a few large private firms devised standard solutions, which led to a proliferation of modern-style, reinforced concrete public facilities across the country. Given the urgency of the situation, design quality, Japan's rich architectural tradition, and regional distinctions were demoted to secondary considerations at best.

By the late 1950s and increasingly in the 1960s, the situation changed. On the inside, a few government agencies, such as the Ministry of Foreign Affairs, began exploring new forms of expression for their buildings, while on the outside, a handful of independent architects, such as Kenzo Tange, started to introduce new approaches to public buildings through works such as the Hiroshima Peace Center.

The 1964 Olympics in Tokyo and the 1970 International Exposition in Osaka were also important turning points in the development of Japan's public buildings. "The Tokyo Olympics of 1964 symbolized the end of the reconstruction period of post-war Japan and the beginning of its rapid economic development," write Hiroyuki Suzuki and Reyner Banham.[2] These events not only yielded public commissions for private architects like Tange, who designed the National Olympic Stadiums and the Master Plan for the Expo, but were also opportunities to upgrade Japan's basic infrastructure. In preparation for the Olympics, for example, new train lines and a network of inner-city expressways were built and streets were widened (Fig. 2). As Japan became more stable and its postwar woes receded into the past, design quality and image began to grow in importance.

By the mid-1980s, image had practically taken over architecture. Design, which had been considered extravagant in the past, became highly sought after during the "bubble" period as a magnet that could draw people and their money (Fig. 3). Japan's economic prosperity stimulated public sector work as well, but many independent architects concentrated their efforts on securing lucrative commercial commissions. As private clients throughout the country paid often exorbitant sums to develop their holdings into eye-catching shops and restaurants or luxurious clubs and apartment complexes, architects of all ages were put to

Fig. 2   Nihonbashi, Tokyo, 1990

Fig. 3
Philippe Starck, architect.
Asahi Beer Super Dry Hall,
Tokyo, 1990

work. "There was absolute freedom of design expression in commercial projects," explains Tokyo architect Toyo Ito, "but expression and appearance became the whole thing, like making a big sculpture."

While many "bubble" period buildings were poorly designed and shoddily built, they opened the eyes of Japanese society to more individual design approaches to private as well as public commissions. "Both public institutions and the general public expressed greater concern for the quality of public architecture, which began to be seen as a means of expression especially emblematic of an information and consumption oriented society," writes architect Fumihiko Maki. "And throughout Japan, public architecture began to depart from a simple functionalism whose aim was to be neutral and easy to use."[3] Of equal importance, the sheer volume of private commissions and clients' insatiable desire for a new vision liberated many young designers from the shackles of an apprenticeship system that all but required them to pay their dues at established firms. Instead, many architects fresh from university landed commissions of their own almost before the ink on their diplomas was dry.

3   Fumihiko Maki, "Public Architecture for a New Age," *Places: A Forum of Environmental Design*, vol. 9, no. 2 (Summer 1994), p. 36.

Japan's economic virility of the 1980s not only spawned a building frenzy but also secured the nation's position as a player in the international arena. As foreign designers flooded Japan's shores in search of juicy commissions, Japanese citizens traveled abroad in increasing numbers, gaining firsthand knowledge of life in the West. Relatively few Japanese architects sought work outside their own country, but the cross-pollination of ideas that accompanied Japan's internationalization was a source of inspiration to architects and their clients, private and public alike.

One of the first government officials to see the potential of architecture as a source of cultural enrichment was the Governor of Kyūshū island's Kumamoto Prefecture, Morihiro Hosokawa. Although a descendant of a powerful samurai clan that had ruled Kumamoto for centuries in the feudal era, Hosokawa made his mark as a politician by advocating change, first as Governor and later as Prime Minister. During his term as Governor, Hosokawa visited the Internationale Bauausstellung (IBA) projects in Berlin – a trip which altered the course of public building in Kumamoto, if not in all of Japan. The IBA's contribution to Berlin convinced Hosokawa that there had to be a better way of making public buildings in his home prefecture. Exploring ways to realize this vision, Hosokawa consulted Arata Isozaki, his friend and a native of Kyūshū.

Accustomed to working in the public system, Isozaki was all too aware that the architect selection system for public works, based largely on connections between big firms and government agencies, excluded young talent. His recommendation was to circumvent the bureaucracy by enlisting designers directly. "If public buildings are commissioned from more talented architects, it will raise the level of architecture in that area," reasons Isozaki. Willing to give it a go, Governor Hosokawa inaugurated Kumamoto Prefecture's Artpolis program in 1988 and appointed Isozaki commissioner in charge of choosing architects. "Isozaki, rather than members of the prefectural government, underwrote the quality of design. This had never happened [before] in Japan," explains Hajime Yatsuka, the Tokyo-based architect and critic, who worked under Isozaki as the director of Artpolis.

Instead of blocks of development, the first phase of Artpolis consisted of some forty individual projects scattered throughout the prefecture. While the aim of the projects, which ran the gamut from public housing complexes and museums to police boxes (Fig. 6) and park furniture, was to have a positive impact on their immediate surroundings, each work was also viewed as a point in a prefecture-wide network. This strategy was particularly well-suited to Kumamoto's largely rural setting, where mountain views and pastoral landscapes are punctuated by small cities, towns, and villages. This loose concept of the whole also freed Isozaki and his team to select a broad range of designers. Though priority was given to young architects suitable to each project, the team did not limit itself to local practitioners, bringing in architects from Tokyo and Osaka as well as from overseas. One architect to benefit from the program was Jun Aoki. A young designer with few built works, Aoki was commissioned to create the Mamihara Bridge (Fig. 4; Plates, no. 1). Located in Soyō Town, a small community in a remote part of Kumamoto Prefecture, the double-deck structure serves as both a tourist attraction and a gathering place for local citizens.

"I am not completely pleased with Artpolis," says Isozaki, "[but] as a model which involves architects in many different types of buildings I am very satisfied." Now in its second phase, Artpolis continues to expand, albeit at a slower pace and with a greater emphasis on cultural facilities owing, in part, to newly elected officials with different agendas. "The new [prefectural] government is hesitant to proceed with public housing projects because it is always a struggle when introducing a new way of living," explains Isozaki.

Eager to enhance their regions, many politicians countrywide have been attempting to follow in Hosokawa's footsteps – Artpolis succeeded brilliantly in turning a sleepy agricultural region into an architectural mecca of international repute. In 1992, for example, when Toyama Prefecture was selected as one of two sites for the annual Japan Expo, Governor Yutaka Nakaoki proposed erecting pavilions throughout his prefecture instead of just at the exposition site. With Isozaki again providing guidance, seven European architects were invited to Toyama to participate in its Machi no Kao (face of the town) program by designing small buildings and monuments (Fig. 5). The aim was to employ a foreigner's fresh vision in creating "faces" or symbols for each town.

Fig. 4
Jun Aoki & Associates, architects.
Mamihara Bridge, Soyō Town,
Kumamoto Prefecture, 1995

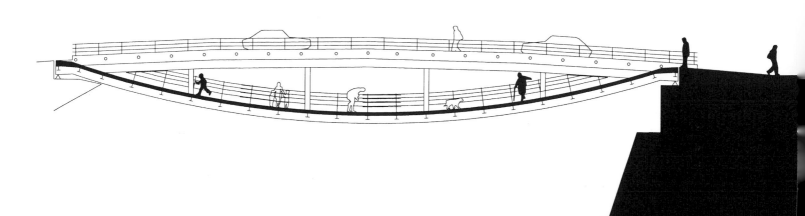

Fig. 5 Ron Herron Associates, architects. Bus waiting area, Daimonmachi, Toyama Prefecture, 1993

Another example is Okayama Prefecture's Creative Town Okayama (CTO), whose twenty-one architectural projects aim to produce not eye-catching, individual buildings but harmonious urban environments as found in many Western cities and towns. "The important thing is establishing a context for the overall appearance and spatial qualities of the environment and then relating architectural design to that context," says architect Shini-chi Okada, CTO's commissioner. And then there is the mayor of Hiroshima City who hopes to beautify his city through the landscape and architectural design projects of Hiroshima Peace + Creativity 50 (P+C 50).

In contrast to programs like Machi no Kao, CTO and P+C 50 represent a shift toward practicality in the planning of many mid-1990s public buildings in Japan. The reasons for this change are myriad. Many recent projects are the direct result of increased public works spending aimed at stimulating the country's weakened, post-"bubble" economy. At the same time, however, government belt-tightening has made it harder to justify architectural experimentation.

One casualty of the new austerity was Tokyo's Bunka Koban (cultural police box) program, which was brought to a screeching halt in 1994 when funds dried up. Most police boxes, tiny police outposts distributed around the city, are designed or commissioned directly by the national Police Agency. The Bunka Koban program, which began in 1983, departed from this pattern by awarding two commissions a year to innovative architects chosen by the program's city-run selection committee. The goal was to

Fig. 6
Manuel Tardits and
Kiwako Kamo, architects.
Kanban Koban police box,
Kumamoto City,
Kumamoto Prefecture,
1995

"enrich the urban environment or make a symbol for the city,"
explains Takeshi Sawaumi, one of the city officials in charge, and
also to improve the image of the neighborhood police officer by
installing him in a striking, but user-friendly, structure (Figs. 1, 7).
Though the Police Agency continues to hire independent architects, gone are the virtually unlimited budgets and avant-garde
designs of the Bunka Koban program.

Instead, many government officials, as well as architects, are
once again focused on practical matters, such as function. For
example, the changing social needs and demographics of the
Japanese population are generating demand for new or expanded
programmatic types, such as buildings that address the requirements of the elderly. "The population of Japan is aging faster than
any on earth, a result of declining birth and death rates," reports
Linda G. Martin.[4] Says Martin, "[b]y the year 2025, nearly one-
quarter of Japan's population will be over the age of 65."[5] As the
tradition of children caring for their aging parents at home wanes,
the need for external, supplemental care facilities grows. Yokohama architect Riken Yamamoto, who has designed both public
and private care centers for the aged, reports that his hometown
alone plans to build some eighty Care Plazas – facilities that meet
the needs of this growing constituency.

At the same time, many small towns are struggling to hold on
to the young, who continue to leave home to live in the big cities.
To stem the flow, many local communities are upgrading, or
adding to, their public amenities. In the past, local bureaucrats
invited industries to set up shop in their communities, hoping
that the prospect of employment would encourage young people
to stay as well as attract newcomers. Today, the incentive is more
likely to be in the form of new schools, libraries, community centers, and arts facilities. In the process, some of the architects of
these buildings are being given the chance to cast aside the standard, formulaic solutions of the past in favor of rethinking programmatic requirements and creating architecture better suited to
the users' needs.

Riken Yamamoto's Iwadeyama Junior High School is a case in
point (Fig. 8; Plates, no. 17). Like many a small community, Iwadeyama fears the consequences of a dwindling population. To
help ameliorate the situation, the town's mayor decided to recast
his rice-cultivating town as an "educational city." And what better
way to inaugurate this new identity than to build a new school!
Atop a hill with a dramatic 330-foot-long metal screen that shields
it from north winds and reflects sunlight inside, the school is
hard to overlook. As the symbol of the new Iwadeyama, the no-
velty of the school is more than skin deep. Known for questioning

Fig. 7 Naoko Hirakura Associates,
architects. Rose Koban, police box,
Tokyo, 1993

4 Linda G. Martin. "The Graying
of Japan," *Population Bulletin*,
vol. 44, no. 2 (July 1989), p. 5.
5 Ibid., p. 4.
6 Yukio Futagawa, interview with
Riken Yamamoto, Tokyo, April
1996, GA Document 47, p. 111.

established programmatic types, Yamamoto devised a scheme that gives form to a new approach to middle school education. "Everything is new," says Yamamoto. "Not just the architecture but also the curriculum and teaching ideology are different from those of schools in the past."[6]

In addition to rebuilding outmoded facilities, many regional governments have been embellishing their territories with brand new cultural and recreational facilities. Isozaki likens this phenomenon to the development of European cities in the eighteenth century. "When the nation states first created their capitals they needed parliament buildings, opera houses, theaters, museums, etc.," he explains. Now that the country's fundamental infrastructure is in place, Japan too is filling in the missing pieces that can raise the quality of life, even in the country's backwaters. Although cultural amenities had long been the dream of many regional communities, these communities simply did not have the resources to build until the 1990s.

Yet Isozaki is skeptical about the benefits of many of these new facilities. "After a little town builds a concert hall in the rice fields they invite a well-known performer for the opening," he says, "but no such musicians come for the next five years. Most of the time it is used for karaoke parties." Hoping to create an arts center that truly contributes to the cultural life of Niigata, a port city on the Japan Sea, architect Itsuko Hasegawa took on the task of programming as well as designing her competition-winning

Fig. 8
Riken Yamamoto and
Field Shop, architects.
Iwadeyama Junior High School,
Iwadeyama City,
Miyagi Prefecture, 1996

scheme for the Niigata Performing Arts Center. After securing the commission, the architect even conducted workshops with government officials and community members to plan for the operation of the six-acre facility. When it is completed in 1998, the center will combine theaters for traditional Japanese and Western performing arts under one egg-shaped roof (Fig. 9; Plates, no. 5).

Another well-planned cultural facility is the Noh Theater in the Forest in the town of Toyoma, where Noh has been performed in local shrine precincts for some 250 years (Fig. 10; Plates, no. 10). The first built component of the town's new master plan, the theater was constructed with funding from the national and prefectural governments that only recently became available. The outdoor stage is situated in the middle of the woods, exposed to the elements like many of its antecedents. Visitors are free to enter the theater and its surrounding sand garden at any time other than during performances. "I think public buildings must be open to the public every day," explains the project's architect, Kengo Kuma.

In addition to tailoring buildings to local citizens' cultural needs, designers are responding increasingly to a site's physical characteristics. Architect Norihiko Dan observes that "more and

Fig. 9
Itsuko Hasegawa Atelier, architects.
Niigata Performing Arts Center,
Niigata City, Niigata Prefecture,
scheduled for completion in 1998

more people are eager to enhance the landscape and urban design in Japan, not only in high density cities but in the countryside as well." This marks a departure from the prevailing practice of paying relatively little attention to site conditions surrounding new public or private projects. This disregard is due in part to the common assumption in Japan that buildings will sooner or later be replaced. If a neighboring structure may be gone tomorrow, why take a design cue from it today? Also, until recently land was so expensive, especially in Japan's major cities, that few clients could afford to attend to the property around their buildings. Today, in the aftermath of the experimental buildings of the "bubble" period, many observers, such as Professor Hiroyuki Suzuki of Tokyo University, believe that there is an even greater need for harmonious development.

Site conditions were an important consideration in Fumihiko Maki's scheme for the Kaze-no-Oka Crematorium in Nakatsu, a city of 70,000 in Kyūshū's Ōita Prefecture. Working with landscape architect Toru Mitani of Sasaki Environment Design Office, Maki incorporated ancient tombs and an existing cemetery into the building's park-like setting. "Together they form a kind of necropolis," explains Maki. There the building stands at the edge of a grassy, oval basin from which the crematorium's octagonal

Fig. 10
Kengo Kuma & Associates, architects. Noh Theater in the Forest, Toyoma, Miyagi Prefecture, 1996

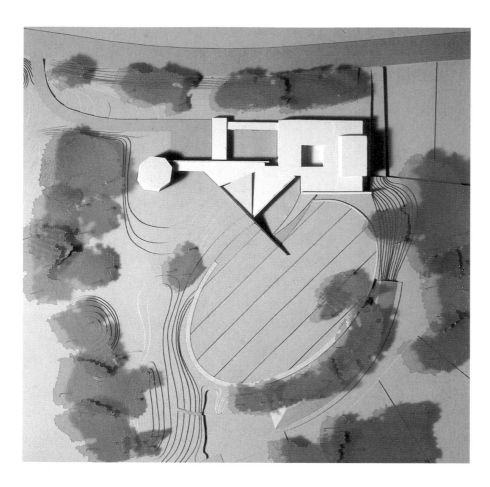

Fig. 11
Maki and Associates, architects.
Kaze-no-Oka Crematorium,
Nakatsu City, Ōita Prefecture, 1997

chapel and corten steel wall emerge like abstract sculptures (Fig. 11; Plates, no. 13).

Even civil engineering projects are benefiting from the growing interest in context. In the postwar period many bridges and dams were built at the expense of natural landscapes or picturesque townscapes. Standardized schemes modified by minor window dressing were the norm. "Many civil engineers have a superficial understanding of what design is," says Norihiko Dan. "They think it is simply something ornamental applied to an already fixed solution." Recently, however, some local authorities have favored solutions that address the particularities of the setting or enhance it. They are increasingly turning to architects to provide these solutions. "People realize that the three ethics of safety, economy, and equality do not equal a better environment," explains Dan, who has been working on the design of the Hiyoshi Dam and community center along the banks of the Katsura River near Kyoto (Fig. 12; Plates, no. 3).

Created as an amenity for area residents who were forced to give up their homes for the dam's construction, the project consists of four components: the community center, the visitor center, the round bridge, and the dam itself, whose internal corridor will double as a gallery. "I am trying to integrate civil engineering and architectural design," says Dan. But melding the different approaches of the two disciplines has been a challenge for Dan, who has had to sacrifice some design control to accomplish the project.

For many independent architects, like Dan, public commissions are a mixed blessing. While government jobs have helped them weather hard times or graduate from small projects to big ones, the work is not without frustrations. To begin with, there is the selection process. According to Dan, some 80 percent of Japan's public building contracts awarded to independent firms continue to be based on a competitive bidding system, in which the architect offering the lowest design fee gets the job. This system has certain merits: it reduces costs and is perceived as a way of curtailing bribery and other unsavory practices, which proliferated in the past. But the system also runs the risk of compromising architectural design quality and knocking smaller architecture firms out of the running, since they may not be able to afford to cut their fees.

Fig. 12
Norihiko Dan and Associates, architects. Hiyoshi Dam's Visitor Center, Hiyoshi Town, Funai District, Kyoto Prefecture, 1995

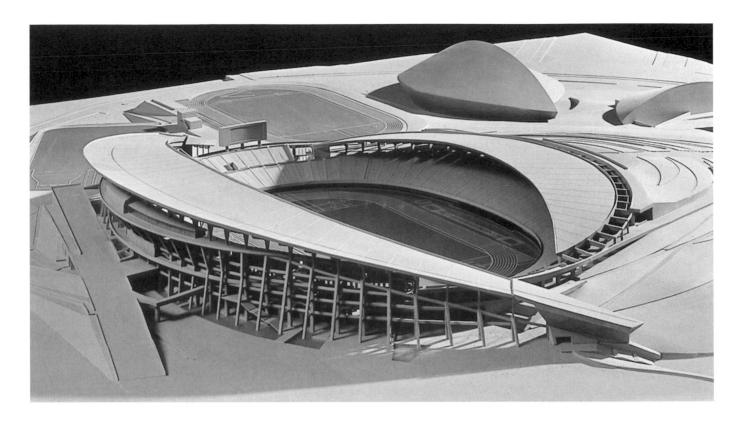

Fig. 13
Haryu & Abe Cooperative
Atelier, architects.
Miyagi Stadium, Rifu Town,
Miyagi Prefecture,
scheduled for completion in 2000

Since the 1980s, various attempts have been made to purge the selection process of unfair practices and open up the market to a broader range of firms. To that end, government bodies have been exploring a whole spectrum of selection techniques, including experiments, such as Artpolis, and competitions of every shape and size. The city of Tokyo has even established a committee whose sole function is to nominate potential architects for its public works. While these new selection methods often help government entities make intelligent choices of designer, they have not been immune to criticism.

Competitions may limit the likelihood of wrongdoing and appear to equalize opportunity, but many are dogged by allegations of selection according to vague criteria or to personal connections. "The design competition is a trial for the jury as well as entrants, and the winning entry is a collaboration by both parties. The jury must clearly identify their standards while going through 100 to sometimes more than 200 entries, which is simply physically overwhelming. Like it or not, the winning entry is an expression of the jury's value judgment," writes Itsuko Hasegawa, who has served on the juries of, and entered, numerous competitions.[7]

Frequently, competitions are judged by committees composed of bureaucrats, academics, local citizens, and practitioners. "Sometimes the committee is just there to rationalize a selection. But a committee also often represents the opinions of the public

7 Itsuko Hasegawa, "Public Buildings and Design Competitions," *The Japan Architect*, vol. 19, no. 3 (Autumn 1995), p. 30.
8 Ibid.

or local citizens. If they are good, it can yield a good product," comments Hitoshi Abe, who was a young designer without a national reputation when he won an open competition to design a new stadium for Sendai, one of the proposed host cities for soccer's World Cup to be held in Japan (Fig. 13; Plates, no. 6). Most competition juries are disbanded once they have reached a decision, leaving the architect to work with local officials, who may not have participated in the selection process or did not even agree with the jury's choice.

The confusion is compounded when there is a lack of clear directives. "The biggest problem of the competitions is programming," says Hasegawa. "Often after the selection, and well into the construction documentation, the inadequacy of the basic concept of architecture or software program, the ambiguity of target users, and the lack of experts' involvement become gradually obvious."[8] Even designers who have not been plagued by programming problems, because they have participated in developments with explicit conceptual agendas like Artpolis or received direct commissions, have had difficulties navigating Japan's bureaucratic morass.

Some independent architects lament that government agencies have been attracted initially to their fresh approach, but later proved unwilling to try something new. In his competition-winning scheme for the Ōta-ku Resort Complex, a combination spa and out-of-town classroom for residents of Tokyo's Ōta Ward, architect Toyo Ito proposed melding the two functional components together inside a single 970-foot-long building (Fig. 14; Plates, no. 8). Thanks to the architect's persistence, he was able to

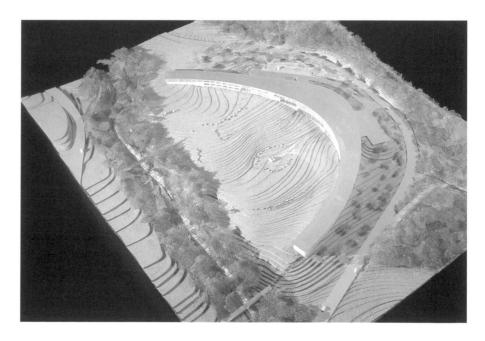

Fig. 14
Toyo Ito & Associates, architects.
Ōta-ku Resort Complex,
Shouken District,
Nagano Prefecture, 1998

overcome government opposition and the design remained largely as planned. "Even when the client is a small town," observes Ito, "it is hard to mix functions within a single building because you must deal with different government offices."

Unlike working with private clients, who usually remain the same throughout a project, working with public entities in Japan often requires coping with discontinuity. As government officials usually rotate assignments every two years, it can be difficult to adhere to the same concepts through an entire project. And then there are the delays, budget cuts, or outright project cancellations that sometimes follow the changing of the guard.

Despite the frequent travails of dealing with Japan's government bureaucracy, many architects enjoy considerable design freedom. "Costs may be closely watched, but no one really controls design quality," explains Professor Suzuki. Architect Yoshio Taniguchi finds public work so rewarding that for the past twenty years he has devoted some 80 percent of his practice to it. "If you have relationships and experience, you can control the work if you are working for the government," remarks Taniguchi, who recently designed the Tokyo National Museum, Gallery of Horyuji Treasures (Fig. 15; Plates, no. 16). Located in Tokyo's Ueno Park, the completed museum will be located near some of the country's most venerated cultural facilities.

Although the volume of new public commissions may be decreasing as the government tackles its perennial deficit by cutting expenditure, the future of public building in Japan looks promising. For one thing, the number of government officials

Fig. 15
Taniguchi and Associates, architects.
Tokyo National Museum,
Gallery of Horyuji Treasures,
Tokyo, 1998

who value design appears to be on the rise. "Now there is a more relaxed attitude from government officials," reports Abe. "They are a little more willing to break away from existing building types." And so, despite economic ebbs and flows, the seeds of change have been planted.

The seventeen buildings illustrated in the present volume are a representative sample of government-sponsored architecture in Japan today. They include a range of building types and settings, and are the products of disparate aesthetic and generational visions. Some of the buildings have been completed recently. The rest are in progress. All point the way to the next millennium.

PLATES: ARCHITECTURE

Note

This portfolio of buildings represents works in the exhibition
that were compiled by guest curator Naomi R. Pollock.
The statements on each project consist of information provided by the architects.
The dates given in the headings refer to actual or scheduled dates of completion.
The wide variety of building types presented in this survey
reflects the sponsorship activities of government entities in Japan today,
be they local or municipal, prefectural, or national.

1   MAMIHARA BRIDGE

Architect: Jun Aoki & Associates
Client: Soyō Town
Location: Soyō Town, Kumamoto Prefecture
Date: 1995

The bridge is located in Soyō, a small community on the southern Japanese island of Kyūshū, which at one time prospered as an overnight stopover for people traveling on the old post roads. However, owing to changing modes of transportation, its raison d'être ceased to exist and the population decreased dramatically, making its almost cosmopolitan hustle and bustle a thing of the past. To help improve this situation, Mamihara Bridge was conceived of as a monument that would serve to attract more visitors to the town.

When architect Jun Aoki was first approached about the project, he had misgivings. Although it seemed to have the potential of bringing the town a certain degree of economic prosperity, he was more concerned about enhancing the quality of life of its residents. He was of the opinion that if such public spaces were aesthetically pleasing and a pleasure to use – that is, if they enhanced the every-day life of the inhabitants – tourists would be drawn to the town as a matter of course. And this is just the approach Aoki took.

Mamihara Bridge is composed of an upper and a lower level. The former is for both pedestrians and vehicular traffic while the latter, the reversal of the traditional Japanese arched bridge, is for pedestrians only. Sheltered from the sun and the rain, this lower level is as much a gathering place as a means of transit. The structure is well integrated into its urban surroundings. When viewing the bridge from the town all one notices is that the road diverges where it spans the river. This is one of the key features of the bridge's design: it is essentially part of the road.

2   OSAKA SUIJO MARINE FIRE STATION

Architect: Coelacanth Architects, Inc.
Client: Osaka City
Location: Osaka City, Osaka Prefecture
Date: 1998

The fire station is located at the center of the Tempozan district, one of the waterfront areas of Osaka's South Port. As part of Osaka City's major redevelopment program, this district is rapidly being transformed from a depressed industrial area into an attractive entertainment district. When the city decided to rebuild Tempozan's old fire station, it asked Coelacanth Architects, Inc. to design a building that would represent the "face" of the district.

The proposed six-story building, with approximately 43,000 square feet of floor space, was designed to accommodate ninety firefighters who work in two shifts, and are sent out both by sea and by road. While the building will serve as a lookout point from which the city will be monitored around the clock, it will also constantly be seen by the people in the city. To emphasize this reciprocal relationship, the windows will be highlighted with red framing.

Unlike the old building, the new one will provide semi-private rooms, instead of one large common space, for the crew on duty. These rooms will be located along the perimeter of the building to allow maximum lighting and ventilation, while being shielded from the streets by louvers. The corridor connecting these rooms will extend, like an arm enclosing the yard, to form a structure that will be used in fire drills.

3   HIYOSHI DAM

Architect: Norihiko Dan
and Associates
Client: Hiyoshi Town
Location: Azanaka, Hiyoshi Town,
Funai District,
Kyoto Prefecture
Dates: Hiyoshi Dam Community Center, 1998
Visitor Center, 1995
Dam and Round Bridge,
1998

Located in a mountainous region northwest of Kyoto, the Hiyoshi Dam is being built to control the water flow into the Katsura River Valley. The Hiyoshi Dam Community Center was commissioned by the town of Hiyoshi and will house an information center, a gallery for landscape art, and sports facilities, including basketball courts and a swimming pool. The center will serve as a new public amenity for those forced to abandon their homes to make way for the new dam, which will benefit the larger communities downstream.

The Community Center comprises two sites, one on either side of the river, which are connected by a narrow footbridge. It is intended to be a "gatehouse" to the dam and, to emphasize this relationship, it bears large, bar-shaped forms that recall elements of the dam itself. Several features of the dam's structure have also been integrated into the design of the complex, such as the watergate and the internal corridor, which will be used as a public gallery. Where the river flows just below the dam, the round bridge will mediate between the new construction and the landscape of a new park. Upstream from the dam, the Visitor Center, which will be used by the dam construction company during construction, will be open to the community once the dam has been completed. The formal continuity maintained between the various facilities and elements of the dam is particularly unusual in Japan, where civil engineers and architects traditionally do not cooperate with one another. It is hoped that the Hiyoshi project will encourage subsequent interaction between the two disciplines.

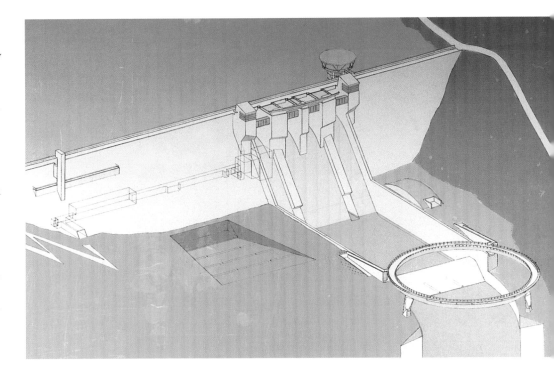

4 MIYAGI PREFECTURAL LIBRARY

Architect: Hiroshi Hara, Atelier Φ
Client: Miyagi Prefecture
Location: Sendai City, Miyagi Prefecture
Date: 2002

Formerly located in an urban area, the main public library in Miyagi Prefecture is now being rebuilt on a site with a varied topography in the center of a newly developed residential district. The library takes the form of a mall-like structure nestled in the natural landscape. The children's reading room and a multi-purpose hall are located on the second floor. An approximately 656-foot-long reading room with a vaulted ceiling is on the third floor. On the exterior of the building, the vaulted roof of the reading room protrudes in two places, where the ceiling reaches some 33 feet in height. Since it is antipicated that the library's collection will be con- siderably enlarged, the design allows for additional stacks over

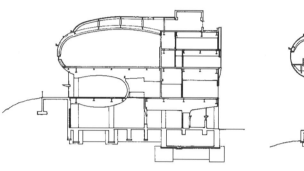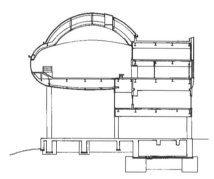

the parking area. The topography has been used to create a plaza suggestive of an open-air theater

that is continuous with the first-floor lounge. The entire terraced site is intended to be a public park.

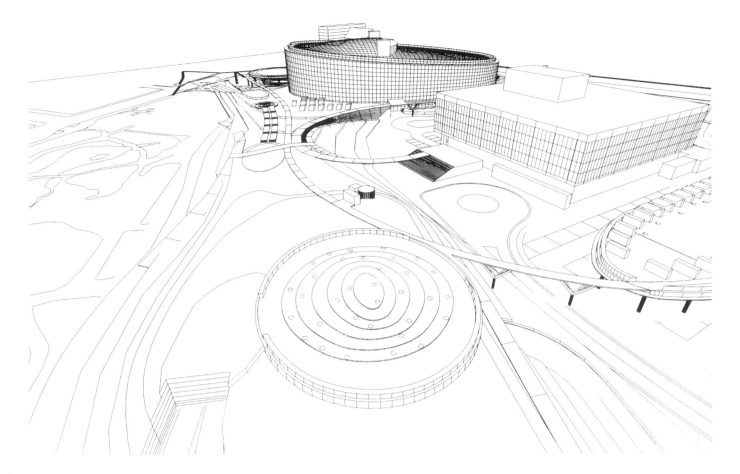

5 NIIGATA PERFORMING ARTS CENTER

Architect: **Itsuko Hasegawa Atelier**
Client: **Niigata City**
Location: **Niigata City, Niigata Prefecture**
Date: **1998**

Reminiscent of the numerous islands that once dotted the Shinano River, the seven man-made "islands" that make up the Niigata Performing Arts Center are laid out in response to complex site conditions. This artificial archipelago has been built on reclaimed land at the same height as the main level of the existing facilities; the islands float among the buildings, engendering new relationships between the public halls, and turning the exterior space into a giant stage.

The main lobby of the new indoor facility is connected with the other islands as well as with the existing facilities by a series of bridges. Above it, a large glass membrane envelops a 1,900-seat concert hall, a 900-seat theater, a 375-seat Noh theater, and rehearsal rooms. By accommodating these three halls in a single volume, it is hoped that a wide variety of interdisciplinary possibilities will be explored, and that new theatrical genres can emerge.

All the facilities in the egg-shaped building employ separate structural systems in order to achieve the greatest acoustic isolation. The roof, where a number of different curved surfaces meet, is covered with a thin layer of artificial soil and grass to form a tilted, green garden.

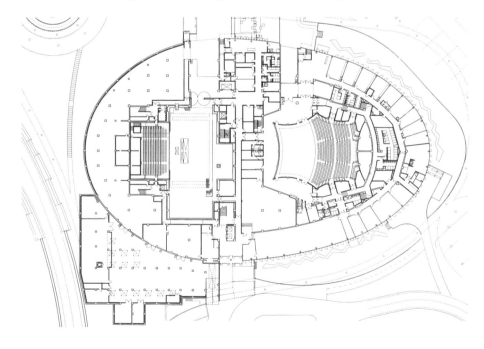

6 MIYAGI STADIUM

Architect: Haryu & Abe Cooperative Atelier
Client: Miyagi Prefecture
Location: Rifu Town, Miyagi Prefecture
Date: 2000

When discussions began about the possibility of Shoichi Haryu and Hitoshi Abe participating in the competition for the 50,000-seat Miyagi Stadium, the former was living in Sendai, while the latter resided in Los Angeles. They thought it would be an interesting experiment to have two architects, so different from one another in age, location, background, and experience, conceive a design together. Their first meeting for the project was held in Los Angeles. They developed the idea through faxes, finalized the scheme, and, upon submitting their proposal, were awarded first prize in Sendai. Today, each runs his own office, and at the same time operates the Haryu & Abe Cooperative Atelier to realize the stadium together.

Abe believes that using standard building types is an effective tool, which architects must use, as a dancer does standard dance steps, but that excessive employment of typologies can result in discouraging the individual from moving freely about a public facility.

Abe's principal interest in designing public buildings is to make building types less rigid. He is of the opinion that they should only be a means to an end, not an end in themselves. Accordingly, Miyagi Stadium combines two typologies: stadium and park. The architects have interwoven these two programs in order to modify the enclosed, centripetal space that traditionally characterizes stadiums, and to create a multifaceted facility.

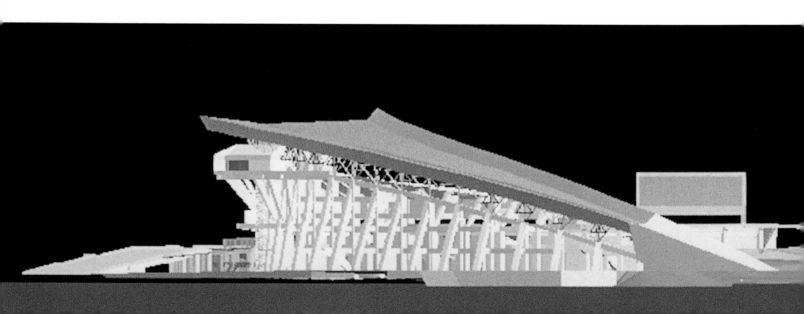

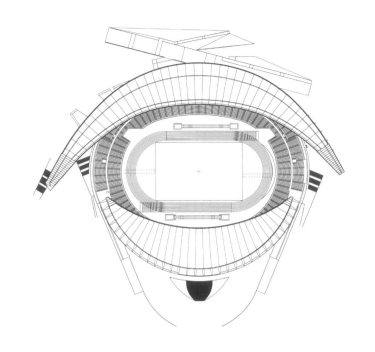

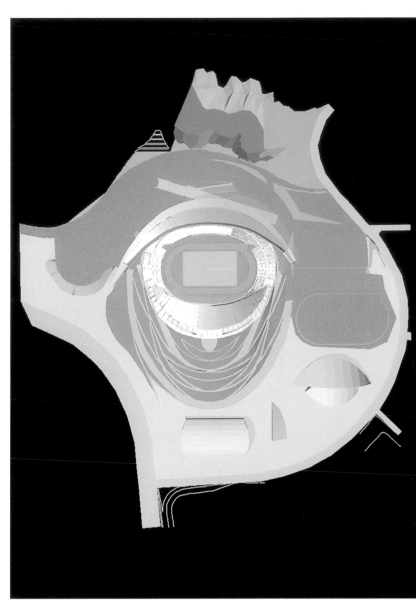

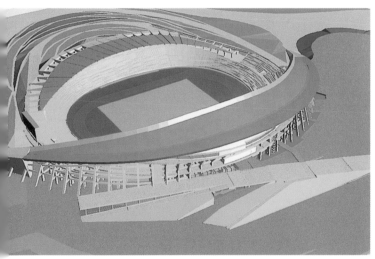

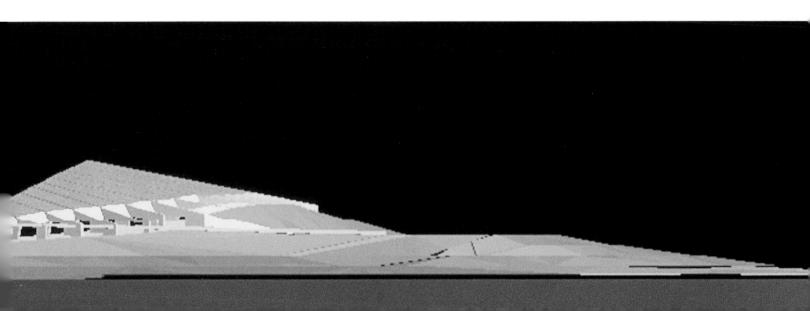

7   OKAYAMA WEST POLICE STATION

Architects: Arata Isozaki & Associates, with Kuramori & Associates
Client: Okayama Prefecture
Location: Okayama City, Okayama Prefecture
Date: 1996

The police station is divided into two sections. The north-facing one is covered in zinc plate and houses the main offices and the prisoners' cells. The south-facing one assumes the same dimensions, but is sub-divided into east and west. The eastern side, which looks directly onto the plaza, consists largely of steel columns. The western side is primarily covered with glass, interspersed with precast Mannari granite tiles, arranged in a checkerboard pattern. This repeats the theme of bisection diagonally. The departments and facilities in this front section are open to the public. They include schools of Judo, Karate, and Kendo, the Traffic Department, and a conference room. The floors in this section vary in height. Where the facade is covered exclusively in glass, and the checkerboard pattern terminates, two distinct surfaces are articulated as a result of overlaying the upper section with a translucent sunscreen.

The steel columns have been reduced to the minimum diameter necessary to support the weight of the roof. Together, they transform the whole eastern volume of the south facade into a space resembling a forest. The checkerboard pattern interrupts the homogeneity of the surface and the regular arrangement of the glass. All the materials used here are fully exposed and were chosen for their diverse and rich textures.

8   ŌTA-KU RESORT COMPLEX IN NAGANO

Architect: Toyo Ito & Associates, Architects
Client: Ōta Ward, Tokyo
Location: Shouken District, Nagano Prefecture
Date: 1998

This project is a resort complex planned by Ōta Ward, a local authority in Tokyo. It combines resort facilities for Ōta Ward residents with classrooms to be used by the ward's public middle schools. The site is in a mountainous region in central Japan near Karuizawa, a well-known vacation spot. A gentle, south-facing slope that was once pasture land, it is divided into eastern and western sections by a stream flowing from north to south.

The some 970-foot-long building forms a large curve that is accompanied by a path on the east side. It is a low-rise with only two or three stories. However, the ground floor is more than 60 feet higher at one end than at the other, and the various segments of the building are linked by ramps, stairs, and elevators. The foundations are made out of reinforced concrete while a steel skeleton constitutes the structural framework of the building – a simple composition arranged in a series of gate-shaped frames. The span of these units ranges from some 36 feet to 104 feet. The largest of them is in the middle of the building, where the gymnasium is located. Generally, the north side is for the use of vacationers and the south side is used by students. However, the building is designed so that it can be adapted to suit different circumstances.

It is hoped that this facility will enable adults and students, who live in the artificial environment of the city, to benefit from its beautiful, natural environment. In order to encourage this, the natural topography has not been altered. The building, which faces away from the mountain was kept quite low to inspire in visitors a feeling of closeness to the earth. Moreover, every part of the structure was made as transparent as possible, making the entire building light and open, and enabling visitors to feel at one with nature. The curved corridors and ramps cause continual and unconscious perceptual shifts owing to their various levels. In moving through the building, the users of this facility are able to enjoy an ever-changing landscape.

9 ARASE BOATHOUSE

Architect: Hideaki Katsura + A·I·R
Client: Sakamoto Village
Location: Sakamoto Village, Kumamoto Prefecture
Date: 1995

Arase Boathouse, a facility for the enjoyment of such water sports as rowing and canoeing, is situated on the shores of the Kuma River. The structure is composed of a boathouse, a control room, an office, study rooms, a training room, and a community room. The two-level corridor, which connects these elements and extends nearly 300 feet along the river, is the most distinguishing feature of the facility. This corridor is not simply a passageway. Integrating the woods and the water visually, it can also be used as a place for spectators or for relaxing by the river. The white silhouette of the building set against the deep green backdrop of the mountains has become the new symbol of the region.

One aim of the project was to erect a structure that utilizes traditional materials and skills but is not unduly influenced by the architecture of the past. Because of the region's role as a harvester of cedar and Japanese cypress and its continuing tradition of timber construction, the building has been made out of wood. Various means were devised in order to create both a highly transparent design

and a structure able to withstand earthquakes and typhoons. Angle braces were used to reinforce horizontal members, and buttresses were installed on the road side to provide the necessary load-bearing capacity.

A battened ceiling, a feature of traditional Japanese wooden structures, was used throughout the building to suggest water, and a narrow, continuous strip of fixed glass was installed where the ceiling meets the exterior wall to let in natural light. Furthermore, columns and braces suggest clusters of trees, echoing the forest outside.

Depopulation and aging are serious problems for Japanese

communities such as this small mountain village. Facilities need to be constructed that create an environment attractive to young people and that encourage settlement. The boathouse was built with this aim and is intended to provide the community with a distinctive space that makes use of the region's natural environment.

Public buildings in Japan have generally been planned by administrative authorities and building experts. In the case of the Arase Boathouse, however, local residents and users, such as people involved in rowing, were permitted to participate actively in this unique project from the planning stage.

10 "NOH STAGE IN THE FOREST" TOYOMA CENTER FOR TRADITIONAL PERFORMING ARTS

Architect: Kengo Kuma & Associates
Client: Toyoma Town
Location: Toyoma Town, Miyagi Prefecture
Date: 1996

"Noh Stage in the Forest" was built to accommodate the performance and practice of Toyoma Noh – a distinctive form of Noh that can be traced back to the late eighteenth century – and to serve as a museum dedicated to this performance art. The aim of this project was to create a space in which Noh could once again be performed in a natural environment. The original objective of a Noh stage was to suggest the natural and supernatural worlds through the arrangement of just two elements: a bridge and a stage. It was not until the Meiji period (1867-1911) that these two features were enclosed in extravagant Noh theaters. In "Stage in the Forest," erected in the woods outside Toyoma, the idea was to return to the simpler structure of early Noh stages and to blend the whole into the forest. This enables the building to be open to the public on days when no performances are given. The town was asked to create a facility that was more a Noh park than a Noh theater. A light, wooden lattice was used for the wall between the town and the building in order to express this open quality, and represents the interface between the town and the "Stage in the Forest." The theater was awarded the Prize of the Architectural Institute of Japan in 1997.

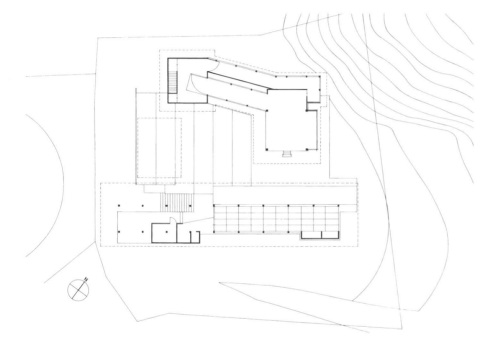

11 FUKUI CITY MUSEUM OF ART

Architect: Kisho Kurokawa
Architect & Associates
Client: Fukui City
Location: Fukui City,
Fukui Prefecture
Date: 1996

The Fukui Museum of Art was designed to provide the people of Fukui City with a place to appreciate art and engage in artistic activities, promoting local awareness of art and culture by realizing Fukui City's goal of "recognizing the artistic legacy of Fukui City and developing it for the future." The fine art exhibition space was to house a permanent collection of works by the late sculptor, Hiroatsu Takada, in addition to a facility for temporary exhibitions and an atelier open to the public.

The site is located on the outskirts of the city, adjacent to a park approximately ten acres in size.

The architecture of the museum was to blend into the greenery of the park, while the park was to be incorporated into the facility as much as possible. The exhibition space is a low structure located in the center of the complex. The museum houses a three-story entrance hall, a cafeteria, and an auditorium.

The entire structure is sheathed in glass, and all the gallery passageways are connected to exterior exhibition spaces and the park, creating an intermediate space between nature and the buildings. Incorporating underground storage spaces into the structure made it possible to restrict the height of the exhibition space to two stories, thereby preventing the building from obstructing the view from the park. The temporary exhibitions are located on the second floor and the permanent collection on the first floor. The atelier is designed so that it may also serve as an exhibition space. The media gallery and the cafeteria enjoy unobstructed views of the park. From the lobby, the second floor can be reached by either a spiral ramp or an elevator, making it easily accessible to the disabled.

12 TŌKAMACHI LIBRARY
Architect: Naito Architect & Associates
Client: Tōkamachi City
Location: Tōkamachi City, Niigata Prefecture
Date: 1999

This project is situated in Tōkamachi, a city of 100,000 located in an isolated mountain valley that receives up to ten feet of snow in winter. The city is known for its production of rice and textiles. Two-thirds of this building's some 35,000 square feet will house the traditional means of information storage, a library, while one-third will contain a computerized information center. The unique character of this project lies in this dual program. Naito Architect & Associates received the commission after winning a design competition, based on their proposal for a "marketplace of information" under one large roof.

Considering the durability demanded of a building in such a location and the efficiency and costs required to maintain it, the architect opted for a flat roof, built to withstand the weight of the snow drifts. Long roof spans were employed to create an open interior space. In order to make the roof sufficiently firm, a post-tensioned, precast concrete construction method was adopted.

13 KAZE-NO-OKA CREMATORIUM

Architect: Maki and Associates
Client: Nakatsu City
Location: Nakatsu City,
         Ōita Prefecture
Date: 1997

The Kaze-no-Oka Crematorium, located in Nakatsu City in southern Japan, reflects to varying degrees Fumihiko Maki's belief that a public building should be a place where people can share their collective memory of a particular time and place. Ancient burial mounds have been incorporated into the public park along with the neighboring cemetery to comprise the crematorium's setting. The focal point of the park is an elliptical green, which dips in the center forming a basin where, as one descends, the surrounding landscape almost disappears from view. Seen from this park, the crematorium appears as an ensemble of abstract sculptural forms set in a natural landscape.

The cremation ceremony is performed according to a procedure that has been practiced for centuries. The sequence of events is of the utmost importance and begins at the moment of the mourners' arrival. It proceeds with the paying of their last respects, which is followed by the cremation of the body. There is then a waiting period, during which the ashes are enshrined and, finally, the process of separation and departure.

This traditional ceremony was the basis on which the design of this crematorium was created.

Consequently, the building consists of three distinct areas: a hall for funeral services, the crematory itself, and a waiting area. Although each element possesses its own distinctive formal character, the spaces are interconnected in order to allow for a natural flow of events. The rooms are enhanced by the presence of natural light, which is controlled through a variety of means. The light that enters these spaces is reflected on the building's assemblage of primordial materials: wood, concrete, corten steel, brick, and slate. The serenity of the setting and the dignity of this ensemble of natural materials and light, makes this complex a memorable place for those paying tribute to their loved ones for the last time.

Entrance to the crematory

The oratory

Pool in the inner courtyard

Waiting area

Enshrinement chamber

The chapel

14 GIFU KITAGATA APARTMENTS

Architects: Kazuyo Sejima & Associates, with Ryue Nishizawa
Client: Gifu Prefecture
Location: Motosu, Gifu Prefecture
Date: 1998 (phase one)

The present design is part of a large-scale public housing reconstruction project commissioned by Gifu Prefecture, and represents the work of five women designers under the aegis of Arata Isozaki's atelier. The idea was to construct the buildings at the perimeter of the site; hence, this block was built parallel to the property line next to the steet. The ground level consists largely of *pilotis* and serves as parking space that may be entered on all sides. One hundred and seven units occupy the second through tenth floors. Approximately one-third of the units are maisonettes. The different apartment configurations have been combined freely in section, generating complex elevations.

Usually, public housing blocks end up being monolithic edifices. By minimizing the depth of this structure, Sejima hopes to create an interesting design for the high-rise block. In addition, each unit has been provided with a terrace, all of which penetrate the depth of the block, creating an irregular pattern of openings, which lends the building an air of lightness. Moreover, each unit is made up of an eat-in kitchen and bedrooms. Silhouettes of the inhabitants moving about inside will be visible from the south, as on a giant screen.

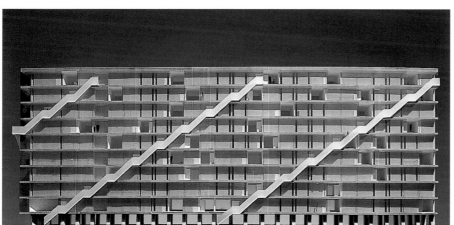

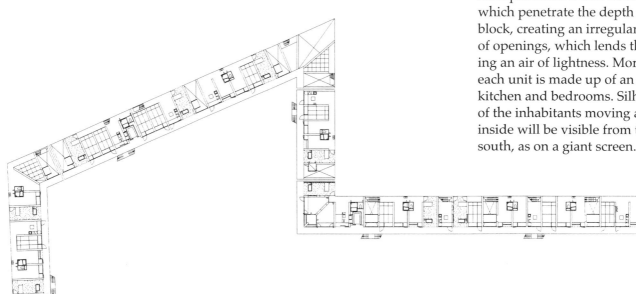

15　KUMAMOTO "BUOYANT CLOUD" STADIUM

Architect: Teiichi Takahashi, Daiichi-Kobo Associates
Client: Kumamoto Prefecture
Location: Kumamoto City, Kumamoto Prefecture
Date: 1997

The basic concept of this project was to design a cloud-like roof over a large space that could be opened up to its surroundings at will. The actual roof is made of a double-layered pneumatic membrane reinforced by a spoke-like configuration of cables. This unique construction, which the architects call a "hybrid," combines positive aspects of both pneumatic membranes and cable structures.

In contrast to most existing pneumatic domes, which must be sealed off so that their interior space can constantly be pressurized to counteract inevitable air leakage, the Buoyant Cloud Dome's pneumatic membrane is a self-contained entity. Only the pneumatic roof requires pressurized air, and since it is supported by columns, the interior can be opened up completely, realizing Teiichi Takahashi's initial image of a cloud hovering over the earth.

The Buoyant Cloud offers various architectural and technical advantages. It does not require artificial lighting during the day, and its central skylight draws external air up and out of the stadium, creating a natural ventilation system. The convex interior ceiling reflects sounds in different direc-

tions, suppressing echoes that are often problematic in large, voluminous interiors. Furthermore, because the Buoyant Cloud Dome's pneumatic membrane is an autonomous structure and does not rely on pressurization to sustain it, its interior is not at risk of collapse from air leakage.

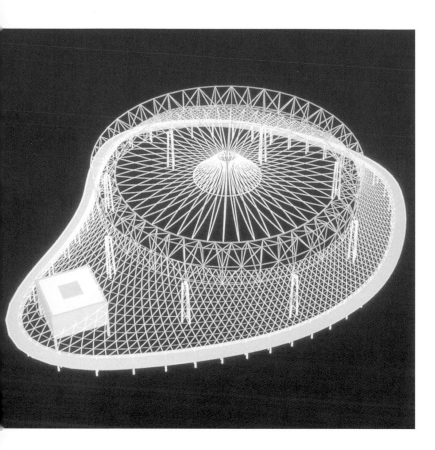

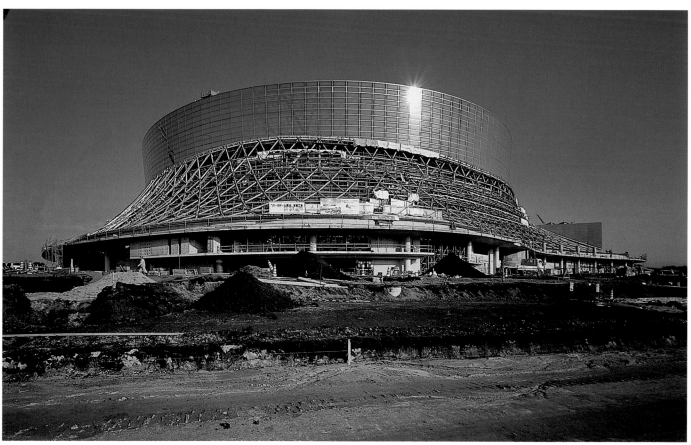

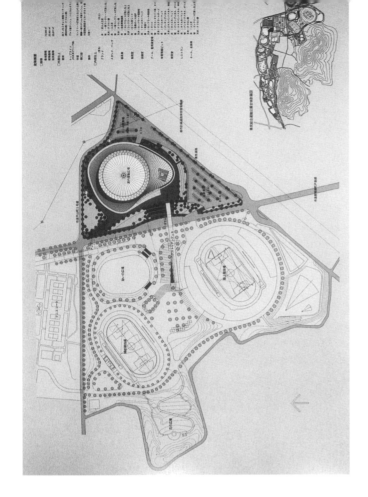

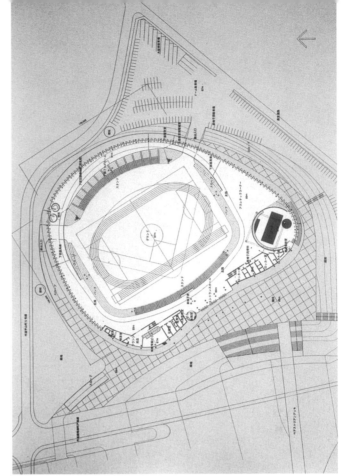

16 TOKYO NATIONAL MUSEUM, THE GALLERY OF HORYUJI TREASURES

Architect: Taniguchi and Associates
Clients: Ministry of Education
and Ministry of Construction
Location: Taito Ward, Tokyo
Date: 1998

This building houses and displays the treasures of Horyuji Temple in the possession of the Japanese government, which includes many valuable national treasures and important works of art.

In order to fulfill the two conditions – preservation and public display – the exhibition and storage rooms have been enveloped by a thick stone wall, while the lobby and lounge spaces, located on the other side of this wall, are glass-enclosed, brightly lit open spaces covered by a canopy. The various layers of the building are meant to recall how the valuable objects inside have been protected and passed down through the ages in boxes within boxes.

As the clients for this project are two government ministries, Taniguchi's approach in dealing with them is to regard them as representatives of the real client – the public. Hence, he wishes not only to fulfill the functional requirements of the program, but to anticipate the public's social and cultural needs, and to create a place where people can experience a unique and enriching environment that stands apart from their daily lives.

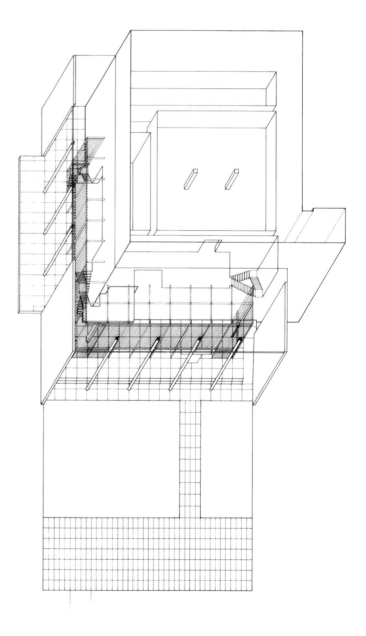

17 IWADEYAMA JUNIOR HIGH SCHOOL

Architect: Riken Yamamoto & Field Shop
Client: Iwadeyama City
Location: Iwadeyama City, Miyagi Prefecture
Date: 1996

In this project, three municipal middle schools were combined to create an entirely new one. Instead of the old system, based on home rooms, the new middle school is organized according to curriculum. This was indicated in the details of the competition brief, and it was obviously the idea of newness that appealed to the mayor of Iwadeyama. It is hoped that this change in the city's educational program will invigorate a city beset by depopulation.

The competition left a great deal to the entrants' discretion. Riken Yamamoto's scheme comprises two domains: the departmental classrooms arranged around the media gallery and an area for everyday student life centered around the atrium, composed of the locker rooms and the multipurpose halls, which the architect named "student lounges" and "student forums," respectively.

The classrooms and teachers' research rooms are located beneath the atrium, on either side of the media gallery. This is a reference room for all departments as well as a workroom for teachers and students, and can be adapted to suit different needs.

In part, because the number of students is expected to decrease by 50 percent over the next decade, the decision was made to use the facility not only as a middle school but also as a cultural and sports facility for the citizens of Iwadeyama. Consequently, Yamamoto proposed arranging spaces, such as music and art rooms, a computer room, a classroom for informing the elderly about health-related subjects, and a shop for wood- and metalwork, around the "Forest Plaza" located on the first floor.

The "Arcade of Light" is located near the school's entrance. Standing here, one can see the gymnasium, the school's entrance, the research rooms, and the soaring "Wing of Wind," both a screen shielding the school from the north wind in winter and a surface that reflects light. In addition, the wall offers a striking landmark when viewed from the Rikuu West Railway Line and the National Road 47 below the hill. Indeed, the hilltop site was chosen in the first place because of its prominence.

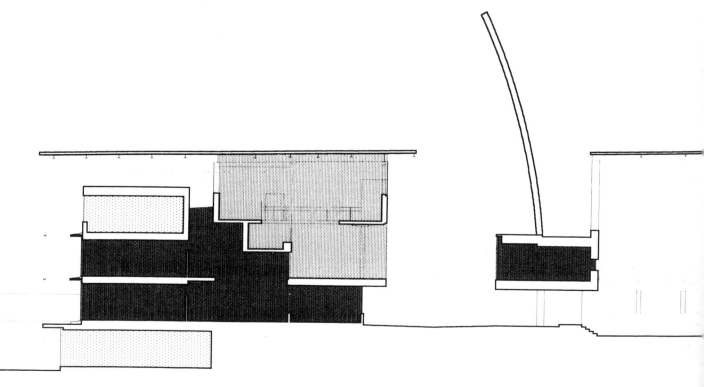

DESIGN

John Heskett The Growth of Industrial Design in Japan

The arrival of Commodore Perry's Black Ships in 1854 marked the end of Japan's self-imposed isolation from the outside world and the point at which a process of modernization began to take place. Under government leadership, the most successful forms of government, administration, defense, and industry were carefully observed, absorbed, and then implemented in a distinctly Japanese manner. Although modern Japanese industrial design is largely a phenomenon of the post-World War II period, it was still characterized by this pattern of assimilation.

Classifying Japanese industrial products in terms of their national characteristics is problematic given the pressures of globalization and the ubiquity of products. For these reasons, it is difficult to associate "Japanese design" with a specific national aesthetic or particular trends in product forms. Nevertheless, design in Japan remains distinctive in terms of processes and values, both of which are heavily influenced by national cultural characteristics. For example, individuality is generally submerged in group identity. Consequently, industrial designers are rarely identified and the origins of products tend to be cloaked in the anonymity of group consensus. Linked to this is the belief that creativity is not only defined by originality, but can also manifest itself in sensitive renditions of past forms – a kind of creative recycling of past ideas. In other words, it is not necessarily what the Japanese design, but how they design it, that is distinctive.

Early industrialization, based on Western models, was primarily preoccupied with developing an industrial infrastructure and military capability. By the early twentieth century, Japan demonstrated technological know-how in such areas as shipbuilding, armaments, and locomotive building. As in other countries, the forms produced by early engineering designers often evinced a strong functional aesthetic. Honed by combat in Manchuria and China in the 1930s, Japanese ships and aircraft performed well against the United States in the early stage of the Pacific war.

The industrial design expertise that existed before World War II derived from European artistic or craft-based concepts, and was centered on the Industrial Arts Institute of Tokyo, a promotional body founded in 1928. The main emphasis was on adapting craft practices to serial production in traditional product categories,

Fig. 1
Mk. 1 Shinkansen train
at Tokyo Station

such as furniture, ceramics, and packaging. The consumer goods industry also emerged during this period, though the products were generally copied from Western models.

Defeat in World War II brought occupation by U.S. troops and enormous change, also in industrial design. For Atsuko Kamoshida, later president of the Japan Industrial Designers' Association, the origins of Japanese industrial design lie in the powerful influence of the American life-style:

> Industrial design was to be seen in all the appliances and facilities at the service of US military personnel and their dependents. Although the concept was not part of the Japanese vocabulary yet, US life style was held in high esteem and was considered as being clean, efficient, and one that afforded comfort and was within the reach of anyone living within a democratic society.[1]

At the time, such a life-style was only an aspiration. Japan's industrial facilities lay largely in ruins but, again, the government took the initiative, by assigning the Ministry of International Trade and Industry (MITI) the task of devising plans for reconstruction and economic expansion based on exports. Its early policies had two main planks: introducing the latest foreign technology and protecting domestic industry while it was being rebuilt. The home market was viewed as a developmental springboard for exports.

Realizing that industrial design had emerged in America between the wars as a field concerned with the marketability of manufactured products, MITI began vigorously to promote it. An advisory group, invited from the Art Center College of Design in Pasadena in 1956, recommended improving design standards in Japanese products and packaging, encouraged the development of design education, and urged long-term goals in developing markets for new products.[2] It was deeply ironic, of course, that just as the example of American design was playing a seminal role in stimulating Japanese design, new methods of financial control and marketing emerging from business schools were already displacing design in domestic American business strategy.

The dilemma for MITI in its advocacy of design, however, was a dire shortage of practitioners. It therefore set out to create a cadre of qualified designers by sending talented young men overseas to be trained. In 1955-56, small groups were sent to the United States, to the Art Center College of Design, the Pratt Institute in New York, the Institute of Design at the Illinois Institute of Technology in Chicago, and to European schools as well. The need was urgent, so by special arrangement the customary four-year undergraduate courses were compressed into one year. The students faced acute pressures and enormous cultural differences.[3] Nevertheless, they learned rapidly and, on returning to Japan,

1 Atsuko Kamoshida, "Foreword," in *Industrial Design Workshop: The Creative Process Behind Product Design* (Tokyo, 1993), p. 5.
2 E. A. Adams, George A. Jergenson, and John D. Coleman, *The Future of Japanese Industrial Design* (Los Angeles, 1957; repr. Pasadena, 1995).
3 For insight into the experience of a member belonging to these first groups, who later became one of Japan's most prominent designers, see Takuo Hirano, "The Development of Modern Japanese Design: A Personal Account," *Design Issues*, vol. 7, no. 2 (Spring 1991), p. 53.
4 *Good Design Products 1990* (Tokyo, 1990), p. 4.
5 Ibid.

were sent by MITI on tours around the country to speak about their experiences. Moreover, leading foreign designers were invited to Japan so that their experience and knowledge could be tapped.

Although it generally refrains from direct action, MITI has taken some decisive initiatives. In 1957, "to promote design activities to produce commodities of legitimate originality,"[4] i.e., original Japanese designs, and also to stimulate public awareness, "The Good Design Products Selection System," popularly known as the "G-Mark" competition, which is still held today, was established. Appointed judges select from between 1,000 and 1,200 products each year. Awards are given for the best product of a given category in each field and one Grand Prize is presented to the overall winner. The award criteria are much broader than those of most other competitions, and emphasize not only appearance, but also function, safety, value or cost, and after-sales service. Consequently, the award has become a respected guarantee of product quality in the Japanese market. Originally restricted to domestic goods, the competition was opened to foreign products in 1984.

To organize the competition, and provide for design promotion on a regular basis, the Japan Industrial Design Promotion Organization (JIDPO), a branch of MITI, was established and has subsequently organized a wide range of national and international design events. Further, to raise the profile of Japanese export products and discourage copying, the "Export Commodities Design Law" of 1959 gave MITI the power to control exports "from Japan in terms of the industrial property rights ... both domestic and international...."[5]

No laws or regulations required companies to employ designers, but the influence of innumerable, informal contacts between bureaucrats and businessmen through which ideas are channeled in Japan cannot be underestimated, and by the mid-1950s, many large Japanese companies had begun to establish design departments. While some new designers returning from overseas were so employed, others set up independent consultancies, such as Kenji Ekuan, who established GK Associates, and Takuo Hirano, who set up Hirano & Associates, which were leading organizations in creating awareness and acceptance of design in the business community. Soon, through new educational courses and on-the-job training, the number of qualified designers began to grow. MITI has continued over the years to view design as a strategic resource for Japan's economy, with ongoing policy reviews providing a framework of ideas and responses to new developments.

Not all initiatives were the result of government action, however, and already in the 1950s the first signs of typical Japanese

approaches to product development were evident in the industrial sector, into which designers were hastily integrated. In areas of early industrial resurgence, such as motorcycles, consumer electrical goods, and photographic and optical equipment, a pattern emerged: variations on product themes were rapidly produced by means of sophisticated manufacturing techniques. Constant, incremental improvement, instead of radical solutions, were encouraged. This was not only a means of reducing risk; cumulatively, it represented a formidable competitive strategy.

It took time for the effects of these developments to become evident to the outside world, but the 1964 Olympic Games in Tokyo clearly signaled a change in perceptions of Japan, with advertising and television programs about the country featuring dramatic images of high-speed "bullet-trains" on the first Shinkansen line between Tokyo and Osaka, opened in 1963 (Figs. 1, 2). These images must have astonished those who still thought that Japanese industry produced only cheap imitations.

Two main factors have marked the subsequent evolution of Japanese industrial design: firstly, the marketing strategies and policies used to implement design in business operations; secondly, designers' views about their trade and its relative merits.

The following are the salient characteristics of Japanese businesses' use of design:

– Strong top-management support for the design department in major companies. A survey published in the journal *Nikkei Design* in 1989 revealed that 80 percent of top executives affirmed the importance of design.

– Collaboration between designers, engineers, and marketers as flexible development teams involved in both long-term product planning and short-term product development.

– Use of off-the-shelf components rather than having everything designed anew. This reduces costs and speeds up development, enabling designers to concentrate on the overall function of the products.

– A continuous flow of information between manufacturers and suppliers, enabling the latter to become involved in the design process, and thereby further reducing costs and development time.

– Long-term investments in new technology and manufacturing and their continual development.

– Continual investment in design education. The Japan Industrial Designers' Association was founded in 1952 with twenty-five members. By 1992, the number of industrial design practitioners had reached 21,000.

The strategies for using design to penetrate both domestic and foreign markets also follow typical patterns, whether the products are automobiles, pocket radios, or ball bearings. From an initial market position, expansion follows four basic strategies, singly or in combination, in an effort to increase market share.

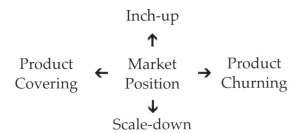

Each strategy requires different design attributes. Product covering is essentially a process of duplicating what is already on the market with minor variations, requiring little more than superficial changes to the product's form and the packaging.

Product churning, especially in consumer electronic products, is a uniquely Japanese approach. In contrast to "rifle-shot" product development in other countries, where efforts focus at an early stage on one specific concept, product churning employs a "shotgun" approach, with designers in parallel teams developing

Fig. 3
Akihabara district, Tokyo

numerous variations of product concepts. The results are then marketed and the public is left to decide which is more appropriate. The central Tokyo district of Akihabara – with its densely packed retail stores in an area of a few blocks accounting for some 10 percent of Japan's annual sales of consumer electronic devices – is where this outpouring of products is put to the test (Figs. 3, 4). A typical example is a range of some fifty vacuum cleaners offered by a single company at one time (Fig. 5). Once a market preference becomes clear, unsuccessful variants are eliminated, and production is increased for national distribution and, later, for export. Product covering and product churning both require a substantial number of designers, although not

Fig. 4
Akihabara district, Tokyo

necessarily highly skilled, and account for the large size of some corporate design departments.

There are occasions when product churning coupled with the flexibility to respond quickly can be a formidable competitive weapon. In a famous case, Yamaha decided to challenge Honda's lead in the domestic motorcycle market at a time when it was already flooded. To counter this move Honda, which like Yamaha normally produced about twenty-seven new models a year, promptly sent its car designers to the motorcycle division, and in 1982 produced forty-five new designs, almost one a week, most targeted at Yamaha's strongest market areas. Yamaha suffered losses that year estimated at some $150 million.[6]

6   Charles Smith, "Why Yamaha Was Forced to Re-Trench," *Financial Times*, Nov. 16, 1983, p. 5.

Fig. 5
Window display of over fifty
vacuum cleaners produced
by the Hirose Company,
Akihabara district, Tokyo

The "inch-up" approach, in contrast, is more sharply focused, with design assuming a strategic role in breaking into higher levels of the market, where quality, distinctive forms, and exceptional service are fundamental requirements. Toyota, for example, entered international markets with small cars developed for Japanese conditions. Gradually, their models penetrated higher-value sectors, a process culminating in the "Lexus" range, which, following its introduction into the American market in 1989, immediately became a best-seller. A key to the success of Lexus was its systemic design approach, with a meticulous design not only of the automobile itself, but also of every visible aspect of the showrooms, sales offices, and service centers.

If Japanese designers have a particular forte, however, it is in "scale-down" strategies, with which they have continually redefined markets. An early example is the Honda "Supercub" of 1958 – still in production today – which reduced motorcycles from the powerful machines that leather-clad males bestrode to a lightweight, small-engined, step-through model, offering inexpensive transportation to people of either sex in regular clothing. The tiny calculators of today derive from a Sharp "desk-top," solid-state calculator, weighing 55 pounds and introduced in 1965. Ten years later, Sony introduced the first VCR for consumer markets, after spending eighteen years developing them from broadcasting equipment, and the famous "Walkman," a miniaturized tapeplayer for portable use. In the early 1980s, Canon similarly scaled-down photocopiers from models affordable only to large businesses, to tabletop models appropriate to small businesses and home use.

It is not only the well-known giant corporations that employ this strategy. In the last four years, a medium-sized firm, Tanita Corporation, which earned its reputation manufacturing bathroom scales, has extended its product line by reducing the size and cost of body-fat analyzers from professional models costing $5,000 to consumer models priced at $200 (Fig. 6). The examples are innumerable, but the result of such ingenuity has been a profusion of products that has continually raised customers' expectations of design and quality.

At the same time, designers themselves have evolved new ideas about their role. Three major trends are discernible: the first concerns expanded ideas on design's role in society as exempli-

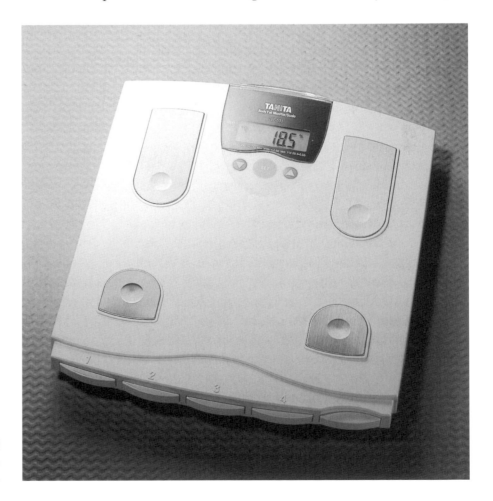

Fig. 6
Body Fat Monitor,
Tanita TBF 531

fied in an MITI policy review of 1988, formulated by heads of design organizations and leading designers. Four key points were emphasized:
– going beyond material levels and contributing substantially to Japan's future quality of life;
– adapting to the latest information technology which introduces new opportunities in industry and in society and makes new demands on design;
– enhancing human and technical potential by combining hard- and software to meet new needs, as inherent, for example, in the changing demographic profile of Japan, with the proportion of elderly people growing rapidly;
– promoting the understanding of design at all levels if its potential contribution to society is to be realized.[7]

Both pragmatic and idealistic, the report combines economic with technological factors, and envisions design redefining Japan's cultural identity in the modern world.

A second trend is the emergence of multi-disciplinary consulting groups offering a wide range of design and planning services. They do not simply execute corporate briefs or design single products, but instead play a long-term strategic role in determining the future of a corporation, its products, services, and systems. An example is the relationship between Hirano & Associates and the CKD Corporation, a manufacturer of packaging machinery. Over a period of thirty years, the firm has emerged from being dependent on overseas licenses to being a world leader in the industry, based on a design policy that shapes every single aspect of corporate activities.

Thirdly, in sharp contrast, is the phenomenon of "star" designers, who project the image of innovative, lateral thinkers. They are independent trendsetters seeking to transcend the boundaries of product concepts and often cultivate a rebel image – and in the context of Japanese culture they are indeed rebels. One such designer, Naoki Sakai, explains: "My product is imagination, dreams, fantasies, desires.... I make human desires."[8] Sakai does not always design products in detail, sometimes suggesting key images and features for others to execute, as in the Nissan "Pao" of 1988. Manufactured only for the Japanese market, this automobile was an example of so-called "retro-design," evoking the forms of the 1950s, and sparked an international trend in creating product forms derived from and recalling designs of the past.

The work of such designers is not strategic but open-ended, exploratory, and symbolic in nature, and the scale on which it has been manifested is yet another distinctive Japanese approach to design. Groups have also been established by major corporations

7   *Design Policy for the 1990s* (Tokyo, 1988).
8   S. Azbybrown, "The Shape of Things: Naoki Sakai Sees Himself as a Designer of Dreams, A Fulfiller of Fantasies," *Winds* (July 1989), p. 54.
9   Leonard Koren, "Corporate Design Strategy: Nissan's New 'Outside' Group," *Japan Design Close-Up*, no. 1 (March/April 1991), p. 2.
10 Frank Gibney, Jr., and Sebastian Moffett, "Sony's Vision Factory," *Time Digital* (March/April 1997), p. 53.
11 Ibid., p. 54.

to fulfill a similar function of generating new concepts, as with the "outside" group set up by Nissan in 1991 in Tokyo "to connect more closely user and maker,"[9] or Sony's design laboratory, which currently employs a staff of forty.[10]

Underlying all these developments, however, is the recurrent theme of how to humanize technology, as summed up by architect and designer Masayuki Kurokawa: "The next era is about the relation between humans and objects. Designers have to make things humans can love and that fit in with their life-style."[11]

Few people in the world remain unaffected by the shift in Japan from producing imitation goods to generating technically superior, well-designed products. In the process, Japan's economic standing in the world and its own standard of living have changed dramatically. Yet, although the achievements of Japanese designers are substantial, a perceptible crisis of confidence among them has become evident in recent times. As in other areas of Japanese life, this stems from the collapse of the "bubble" economy in 1992, largely owing to speculative policies by major financial institutions, that sent shock waves through Japanese society. The annual growth rate of design services of nearly 9 percent prior to 1992 has fallen drastically, resulting in serious cutbacks and some design consultancies going bankrupt. Widespread soul-searching is evident on several levels. There are efforts to develop sophisticated design methodologies capable of handling the complexities of modern technology. In commercial contexts, there are problems with foreign competition in today's global market. Conversely, there is the desire to move beyond the uniformity of global products and to evolve forms truly expressive of Japanese culture and tradition. Another persistent note calls for more "emotional" approaches to design, free of commercial pressures.

The future evolution of Japanese industrial design seems likely to follow multiple paths, but it is precisely the vigor and diversity of debate and the new roles they envisage for themselves in Japanese society that is perhaps the best evidence of the distance Japanese designers have traveled since the 1950s. Design, however, is innately focused on the future and, if current aspirations to humanize technology are realized, Japanese designers could exceed their past achievements and make an even greater contribution to the lives of people across the globe.

Takuo Hirano The History of Japanese Design: A Personal View

The history of design in Japan begins after 1945, following the country's defeat in World War II. Prior to that, traditional Japanese crafts and motifs as well as advertising posters existed, but there was no industrial design, in the contemporary sense, closely associated with the manufacturing sector.

During the early years of the Meiji period (1867-1911), Japan cast aside its policy of isolation from Western countries and opened itself up to the outside world, and in the 1860s eagerly began "importing" culture from overseas. It was state policy to reward individuals and businesses that could make and produce products similar to those made abroad, and that pattern continued to dominate Japanese industry for nearly a century, until 1945. Throughout this long history, the Japanese did not consider it wrong to imitate the design and manufacture of goods produced in other countries. In fact, the better the product, the more they believed it worthy of being emulated and copied (Figs. 2-4). After the war, when Japan's economy and industry began to develop with unexpected speed and the country started to export products to other countries, it was not long before there were movements abroad to boycott Japanese goods.

In 1946 and 1947, when raw materials for manufacturing were not available, the Japanese gathered together what machinery they could salvage from bombed factories and used the tin cans and glass bottles discarded by the occupation soldiers to make small toys and articles of daily use. By the beginning of the 1950s, Japanese industry had revived and was growing at an extremely vigorous rate. Manufactured goods began to improve in quality and to be exported overseas, where they were favorably received. While it was said at one time that only one Japan-made cigarette lighter in ten would work, production technology gradually advanced to the point at which Japanese lighters were reliable. The price, moreover, remained low. Thus, Japanese products ceased to be "cheap and of poor quality" and came to be known as "cheap and of high quality."

In the countries to which Japan exported, of course, this meant trouble for local industries, which found they had to struggle to stanch the influx of Japan-made goods. In those days, the Japanese government was kept busy warning businesses against unfair

Fig. 1
Takuo Hirano (lower right)
teaching design at the Tokyo
National University of Fine Arts
and Music, 1958

trade practices infringing on American design rights and copyrights, and settling disputes over plagiarism and fraudulent use of design ideas.

As mentioned, the Japanese saw nothing wrong in using others' ideas or designs. The Japanese government realized that it would be unable to solve this fundamental problem by enforcing strict controls. In 1955, they selected four working designers who were art school graduates and sent them to study in the United States, Germany, and Italy, thus acting on a policy of importing modern design concepts and technology into Japan.

I was one of those students. I studied at the Art Center College of Design in Pasadena, California, and upon my return, I was assigned the task of establishing the fundamental principles of design education at the Tokyo National University of Fine Arts and Music, Kanazawa College of Art, and the Women's College of Fine Arts in Tokyo. At each of these institutions, the seeds of design-related education had already been planted, but there was much confusion and hesitation about how to develop them and, in particular, what kinds of courses to create.

At the time, I believed that there should be some clear standard for distinguishing between a work of creative design and a work of imitation. My proposal, submitted to the Ministry of International Trade and Industry as a strategy to promote design, is what is known today as "The Good Design Products Selection System."

In the mid-1950s, Japan learned not only about design from America, but also about technology and market research. The Japan Productivity Center was established with the support of both the Japanese and the U. S. governments to spearhead various educational and information programs aimed at raising industrial productivity. Under the auspices of this organization, many

Fig. 2
Left: imitation perfume bottle, produced in Japan; right: original bottle of Diorams, Eau de Cologne, Christian Dior, France

Fig. 3
Left: imitation of the
German model, made in Japan;
right: motorcycle, made in Germany

engineers and specialists studied or engaged in research in the United States. They acquired much valuable knowledge of new types of technology and related control systems, which they brought back to Japan and applied to great advantage in Japanese industry. They were also able to develop effective methods of market research.

Japanese industry, which was then rapidly gaining momentum, thus began to move forward with great strides, guided by the design, technological, and marketing knowledge and skills acquired from the United States. The problem was that, because of Japan's history, individuals in Japanese industry did not have a firm understanding of modern design, and continually tried to judge design as they did technology and market research – in numerical terms. The impossibility of evaluating design on the basis of numerical criteria led those involved in the manufacturing industry to avoid becoming involved in design-related matters regarding merchandising and product development. It became the custom to carry out merely the most superficial kinds of design work – limited to shape, color, or decoration – only after product planning or merchandising had been completed and almost entirely on the basis of technology and market research. This custom led to the status of Japanese designers, 90 percent of whom were in-house designers, falling below that of technicians

Fig. 4
Left: imitation of the German model,
made in Japan; right: camera, made
in Germany

and market-research specialists, and it became accepted practice to assign designers, or design units, to the technology or market-research divisions of companies. Because of their low status, designers were content when their smallest suggestions were taken into account and were reflected in the products. It was not uncommon for a company to make its market-research departments responsible for generating new ideas for products. The necessary data would be collected and a rough model created. Only then would the design department come into play, to perform the job of creating templates based on the rough model.

In this process, the products being planned were based on data collected at about the same time and in the same place as that gathered by other corporations. The data was therefore practically identical, resulting in products that were extremely similar, even though the companies were rivals. This was why Japanese electrical appliances, automobiles, and even textiles looked much alike (Figs. 5, 6).

This close resemblance among products was not an issue in the domestic market. But when Japanese products were found to look very similar to products made abroad, problems arose. For example, a leading radio manufacturer learned that a Dutch-made radio of a particular style was selling well in Europe and began to study and reproduce this product. In no time, several other Japanese manufacturers followed suit and, in a very short time, a vast quantity of new products were created in roughly the same design as the Dutch company's original and placed on the market. This flooding of the market with Japanese imitative export products was severely condemned.

This unfortunate situation was the result of the fact that market research was held to be more important in Japanese industry than design. It was not surprising that Japanese manufactured

Fig. 5
Left: imitation textile, produced in Japan; right: original textile, produced in Japan

Fig. 6
Left: imitation textile, produced in Japan; right: original textile, produced in Japan

goods created on this basis should end up arousing ill feelings in various parts of the world.

In the 1980s, the United States and European countries put pressure on Japan to focus on domestic demand. When industries that had turned out merchandise for world markets shifted to the domestic market as an outlet for their products, Japan became awash with consumer goods within half a year. Satiated Japanese consumers' interests moved rapidly away from material wants, focusing on leisure and cultural pursuits that offered greater satisfaction and enrichment.

Japanese industry faced the urgent question of what it should be making. After much vacillation, manufacturers began to move in the direction of creating and producing goods with higher value-added features than those made previously. But even as this new trend took shape, three major structural challenges arose in its path: the collapse of the over-heated "bubble" economy, the rise of the information industry prompted by the rapid development of computers, and the dynamic economic development of China and the nations of Southeast Asia.

These three developments emerged just as Japanese industry, prompted by the shift in consumer desires, was beginning to move away from its market-research-led approach to produce value-added goods on the basis of a three-pronged design, technology, and market-research approach. As a result, tremendous structural changes have been forced on Japan in social institutions, in industry, and in education. Today, a new kind of paradigm shift is required for Japan as a whole to renew and reinvigorate itself. This provides an excellent opportunity for the Japanese economy to rebuild itself. It can do this, for example, by creating a new type of industry that combines the hardware-centered technology available in Japan with new kinds of software, such as is available in multimedia technology. The effective forging of such a combination cannot happen without vigorous input from designers. The time has come, moreover, for new fields to emerge and to stimulate the interfaces between industry and the environment, information and education, and industry and culture.

The present selection of works, which represents the positive aspects of the history of Japanese design, is significant and interesting in itself. It is my hope, however, that viewers will also gain an understanding and appreciation of the background from which these works have emerged.

Tadanori Nagasawa The Cultural Engineering of Traditional Local Industry

The Transformation of Daily Life and Japanese Products

Broadly speaking, two categories of Japanese products are known around the world: one encompasses household appliances, audio-visual equipment, automobiles, and other products produced and exported by large, modern manufacturers; the other includes handcrafted products rooted in the ancient tradition of Japanese arts and crafts. It was only after World War II that Japan began seriously to develop modern industrial products using industrial design methods tailored to mass production. Naturally, they mainly conformed to Western design methods, and the resulting products were of a standard worldwide type (Figs. 2, 4, 5). When people speak of modern Japanese industry, it is generally this type of advanced industrial product they have in mind. However, part of modern Japanese industry is what is known as "local industry" (*jiba sangyo*). While this includes small-scale, mechanized industries developed at the end of World War II, it also refers to the manufacture of products made with traditional technology, following an integrated process in which the individual artisan is responsible for all phases of production – from the design to the final stages – in what can be called "machine-assisted handmade" manufacturing (Fig. 3). Despite the fact that these, too, are industrial products, it is still possible to make a distinction between them and what, today, we would call mass-produced, industrially designed products.

Because of the appeal of the novel or the exotic (i.e., a first-hand encounter with another culture), traditional arts-and-crafts objects included in exhibitions as introductions to Japanese culture are particularly eye-catching (Figs. 6-8). Speaking from my own experience, most people in other countries (except for the few who are familiar with Japan) do not really understand what modern Japan is all about. The Japanese themselves, on the other hand, tend to emphasize only certain aspects of Japanese culture; they might, for example, show their foreign friends how to fold origami, or give them traditional handcrafted objects as presents. This being so, it is not surprising that Mount Fuji, geisha girls, and top-knotted samurai hairdos continue to be dominant images in the minds of non-Japanese. Also, in an apparent effort to make things easily comprehensible to their audience, the mass media

Fig. 1
Entrance to a typical, modern Japanese home

Fig. 2
Takenobu Igarashi, designer.
Tableware, Tsubame shinko Kogyo

overseas often focus on aspects of Japan that are far removed from everyday reality and therefore unfamiliar even to native Japanese. Another factor is the paucity of information coming out of Japan itself, in part, because of the language barrier. When portraying Japanese culture, it is all too convenient to fall back on photogenic images of temples and shrines, gardens, traditional cuisine, living environments that include tatami mats, shoji screens, and fusuma partitions, or on traditional arts, such as Kabuki, Noh, sumo wrestling, the tea ceremony, and flower arranging. In this day and age, however, such traditional Japanese images are exotic to the Japanese themselves.

Fig. 3
Lunch-box, Oodate Kogeisya

Fig. 4
Digital camera, Casio

Most attempts to introduce Japanese culture abroad thus focus on aspects of art and culture that are far removed from the every-day life of ordinary Japanese people. Projects that introduce foreign audiences to the realities of modern life in Japan have been rare. Because the idea is to introduce culture, attention tends to focus on the most refined expressions of Japanese artistic culture, and that is usually equated with the traditional culture that matured over the centuries and represents an indigenous, uniquely Japanese development.

But today's Japanese wear Western clothes, enjoy the cuisine of many different ethnic groups, and wear kimonos only on rare

Fig. 5
Matsushita, designer.
Television set, Panasonic

Fig. 6
Wooden Package Exhibition '85
at AXIS, Tokyo

Fig. 7
KIRI Exhibition '94
at COLLEZIONE, Tokyo

Fig. 8
KIRI Exhibition '92
at AXIS, Tokyo

Fig. 9
Contrast between old and new
in a typical Japanese town

occasions, if ever. Most homes have sofas, chairs, and tables just like any Western home, and household menus include not only Japanese but also Western- and Chinese-style fare as a matter of course. Although many people do go to Shinto shrines to pay their respects at the New Year and on other occasions, they also celebrate Christmas, albeit in a rather secular fashion. Young people nowadays prefer to wrap their presents with paper and ribbons in Western style, and see nothing incongruous about fast-food restaurants serving hamburgers and pizzas in a Japanese environment (Fig. 9).

All this is the result of the concentrated effort that has been made to acquire the tools and equipment needed to support the sought-after Western life-style, which has always symbolized modernization for the Japanese. The food they eat and the places they live in now incorporate elements of both Japanese and Western origin, and it is clear that the traditional life-style of old Japan has begun to break down. This tendency is growing increasingly pronounced in urbanized settings, particularly among the young, and is also having a strong impact on traditional arts and crafts. The fact that Japanese life-styles have changed means that Japanese culture has changed.

That is, changes in the way people conduct their lives have engendered changes in the tools and equipment they use. This, in turn, has created a crisis in traditional arts and crafts, which mainly exist to produce articles and implements for a traditional life-style that is becoming increasingly less viable.

The Decline of Traditional Local Industries

Most of the traditional local industries operating throughout Japan originated in the Edo period (1603-1867) and have become indispensable elements of their respective local cultures. Many of these traditions were started in early modern times, when local lords invited urban artisans (from Kyoto and elsewhere) to set up shop in their domains. Many of these arts and crafts, including ceramics, metal casting, lacquerware, metalwork, woodworking, papermaking, and weaving, are considered quintessentially "Japanese" by Japanese and foreigners alike.

Although the scale of production is not large, these enterprises still serve as valuable cultural resources in their respective communities, and they impart a distinctive character to local industry. Originally, they were not always located near the sources that supplied them with raw materials. In fact, the way in which the relationship developed was often reversed. Such suppliers of raw materials emerged after the enterprise in question had been transplanted by a local lord, and became established over the course of time. Some of these enterprises could be situated only in certain places because of Edo-period trade routes or such climatic factors as humidity or temperature.

Most of the products made by these traditional industries depended in some way on traditional Japanese culture and filled both functional and aesthetic needs. With the changes introduced by modernized life-styles, however, it became impossible to cater to a sizable market without product styles being altered to suit modern needs. Meanwhile, traditionally handcrafted products, which tend to be labor-intensive and require a great deal of technical training, are losing their ability to compete against the widespread efforts being made to improve industrial productivity and to reduce manufacturing costs by means of developing new materials and innovative production technologies. Daily needs can now easily be met by inexpensive, mass-produced products. If the modern consumer wishes to meet those needs with high-quality, handcrafted products, he or she must first have access to considerable financial resources, even before the question of taste comes into play. Thus, we find that, while the cultural value of traditional crafts is widely acknowledged, this does not necessarily translate into actual purchases.

I believe that the preservation of traditional craft techniques is equivalent to protecting culture. If traditional industries are not economically viable, however, it becomes difficult to transmit these techniques to succeeding generations. Unless national and local government recognizes the cultural significance of the techniques and acts to preserve them, regional production of traditional crafts will decline. The nature of Japanese life has changed in the wake of postwar modernization and industrialization, and the changes that have occurred in Japan's traditional life-style have led to the diminished distinctiveness of Japanese culture.

Another serious problem is the lack of young people willing to carry on the craft traditions. The apprentice system (which has always provided the basis for transmitting traditional skills) holds little attraction for today's computer-oriented generation, which feels that the modest economic rewards do not justify the physically and mentally demanding training they must undergo. This is, no doubt, a global phenomenon.

Many changes have, in fact, occurred, but they do not mean that Japanese life has been completely Westernized, or Americanized. Nearly all Japanese still remove their shoes before entering their homes (Fig. 1), and Japanese food still holds the central place in their diet. The custom of bathing outside the tub and soaking in the bath for warmth and relaxation is another uniquely Japanese tradition that survives. Even Japanese clothing has not been completely abandoned. Nearly all families have both Western and Japanese tableware and freely combine chopsticks with knives and forks.

Japanese enjoy coffee, pekoe tea, and Chinese teas as much as the indigenously grown green tea, and they love not only rice, but also bread and many kinds of noodles. They consume a wide variety of fish, shellfish, and vegetables, as well as many different kinds of meat. Even without going to a so-called "ethnic" restaurant, the diet of a Japanese family is quite cosmopolitan, incorporating Western, Japanese, Chinese, and other Asian-style dishes.

Unwilling to give up their tatami, but equally fond of sleeping in beds, people no longer have any compunction about sleeping in a bed in a room covered in tatami matting – a phenomenon that has grown pronounced enough to inspire the marketing of beds designed specifically for that purpose. I believe these examples represent the life-style sensibilities of the Japanese today. Their eclecticism is observable in religious matters as well. Marriage ceremonies may follow either Christian or Shinto ritual, but funerals are usually held according to Buddhist tradition. As in Western Europe, where the popularity of Sunday church attendance has declined, Japanese religious sensibilities are not as strongly rooted in observance of ritual as they once were.

While it is not my intention here to discuss modern Japanese culture, my own speculation leads me to the inevitable conclusion that the Japan imagined by Americans is quite different from the actual life-style of today's average Japanese. In the fifty years since the end of the war, a new Japanese style has emerged in the way people conduct their lives and in the accessories and implements they use. This new style consists of elements that have been hungrily incorporated from many other countries and arranged in a distinctly Japanese manner. It touches on all aspects of human life, including clothing, food, and housing. The eclecticism of the style might well be considered the defining characteristic of Japan's new culture.

The Role of Designers in Japan's Modernization

Designers have made an immense contribution to the modernization of Japan and have played a major role in bringing about the current diversity of Japanese style. The design profession that emerged after the war operated on a basis that was entirely different from that of traditional craftsmen. It evoked a progressive image, for design was a driving force behind mass-production systems in Japan aimed at the establishment of an industrialized state as well as the modernization of Japanese life-styles. Poor in resources, Japan had only one way to extend its economic power: by improving the quality and design of its products and enhancing its international competitiveness through trade. In pursuing this goal, there was no question that an internationally acceptable style of design was preferable to a distinctively Japanese one. It is true, however, that this policy had an adverse effect on traditional Japanese styles. Of course, commercialism had a strong impact too. To the Japanese, modernization meant Westernization, so it is not an overstatement to say that Japanese designers contributed to the physical embodiment of this Westernizing trend in Japanese lives.

Because designers give "form" to concrete things, they are constantly thinking about the meaning of "form." This is a philosophical act that fosters ethical concerns. Designers must respond to ecological issues, find ways to conserve resources, give consideration to safety, determine whether or not the object being designed is really necessary, and think about "culture." These and other activities, which might be called "designership," provide the main premise for their work. Until now, industrial development around the world has focused almost exclusively on economic profitability and efficiency, and is clearly related in some way to the demise of localized, traditional craft production. Now is the time to put "designership" to work to remedy our current situation. If nothing is done, the skills that represent the concrete, living cultural resources so prized by local communities will die out, and the treasures of local distinctiveness will vanish.

Now that the life-style of the Japanese people has changed, it is no longer possible to preserve the original form of the traditional processing technologies and crafts that still exist in local communities. Of course, the use of the adjective "traditional" implies a conservative attitude dedicated to preserving the methods and practices handed down from ancient times, and it is precisely because of this attitude that the traditional crafts have been preserved in the first place. Unless new ideas and design concepts are introduced, however, it will be difficult to find a solution to the current predicament. However, a total revamping of these industries is not the answer either, since that would do away with the traditional elements and destroy the cultural value that people are struggling to preserve and maintain.

Furthermore, a balance must be struck between maintaining an acceptable industrial scale and preserving an appropriate level of regional exclusivity; otherwise, the cultural distinctiveness of the local industry in question runs the risk of being lost. Tradition is analogous to culture, and though it is easy to destroy or ignore it, we would all be susceptible to cultural impoverishment if tradition were allowed to die out. Following the flow of modern civilization, all the world's advanced industrialized nations make basically the same products. One way that Japan might generate a new, distinctive industrial culture within the framework of today's globalized economic and productive systems would be to restore originality to its products. There is more to Japan than the Tokyo metropolitan area. Although Tokyo may be a cosmopolitan city, in which foreigners can enjoy conveniences and comforts familiar to them, the industrial culture that supports Japan's unique traditions is not found there, but rather in rural areas throughout the country.

A New Relationship Between Designers and Local Traditional Industry

Young designers have begun to experiment with new ways of using local, traditional techniques and materials (see Plates, nos. 33-42). Attempts had previously been made, with government assistance, to develop traditional crafts and local products. These efforts were primarily focused on shaking up traditional conservatism and providing guidance for improving productivity and achieving economic and industrial modernization. While this did have a relatively positive effect, it is also true that modernization and improved efficiency have contributed to greater standardization and a loss of regional character.

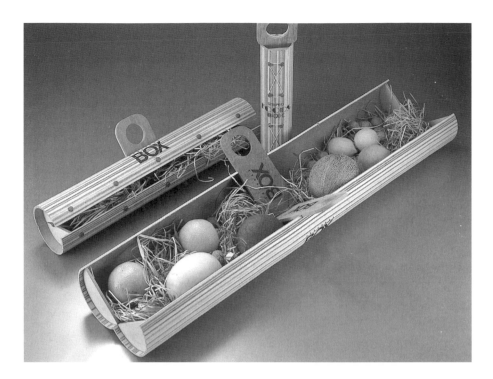

Fig. 10
Hiroyuki Okada, designer.
Wooden package

What sets today's young designers apart from their predecessors is that they start by paying close attention to the distinctive characteristics of the regional industries they deal with. The crucial point is that they have no desire to change the industries themselves. Rather, their goal is to familiarize themselves with a given industry's history and special qualities, and to develop designs that will take advantage of its resources, i.e., its traditional techniques and materials (Figs. 10-12). In this way, they hope to use traditional materials and processing technologies to create things that are more in tune with what they perceive as the new Japanese life-style. They are looking for inspiration from traditional industrial culture and attempting to extract new possibilities from it. Within this traditional culture, it is not customary to pay design fees; in fact, design is a service virtually free of charge. Hence, traditional craftsmen cannot assess the value of their own technologies and know-how, and cannot keep up with the times by spontaneously developing new designs. The young designers understand this. They do not consider themselves on a mission to reform traditional industries, they simply want to design things that can be made with traditional resources. I scarcely know what to call this attitude, but I believe the individualistic, unsentimental approach that has been adopted by the young generation is something that has never been tried before.

It is precisely because traditional craft techniques and materials are "traditional" that they do not change in response to reform efforts forcibly applied from the outside. Although production

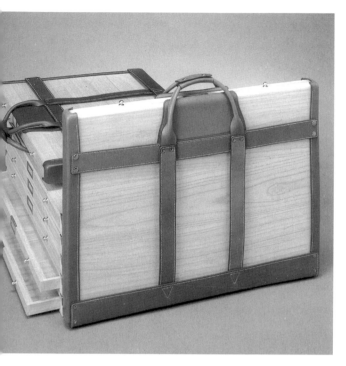

Fig. 11
Keiichi Takenaga, designer.
Wooden cases

Fig. 12
Ryuya Aoki, designer.
Wooden boxes

centers for traditional technologies and materials no doubt *have* changed when viewed historically, they neither have the strength nor enjoy the conditions necessary to resist the drastic changes that have occurred recently in Japan's industrial structure and economy. The young designers' involvement is an attempt to salvage viable products and to secure them a place within the new life-style of modern Japanese. It seems to me that, if the traditional production centers themselves awaken to this new culture, they will find a way to balance progressive development with conservative preservation. I would call this a new "cultural engineering" approach to traditional craft production centers. Even if the production centers themselves are reduced in size, their traditions will gain the protection they deserve, and we could well see the development of a popular movement aimed at retaining regional industrial culture for its symbolic value. In this, I can discern another way in which designers can play a meaningful role in local culture. Through their experiments, it is my hope that a new Japanese originality will emerge.

PLATES: DESIGN

Note

The following entries were compiled by Tetsuyuki Hirano and Tetsuro Hakamada
with a view to placing these products in the context of contemporary Japanese society.
The objects featured are either mass-produced, mass-marketed products or ones
produced in limited numbers that rely, in part, on craft tradition. The mass-produced,
industrial objects were selected from G-Mark winners of the past several years.
The G-Mark awards program, established in 1957 as a means of upgrading Japanese
industrial production by encouraging well-designed products principally for export,
has recently entered a new phase. It now intends to promote design as an integral
component of the domestic market in a drive to lead Japan into the next millennium.
The tradition-oriented objects provide a telling contrast to the G-Mark winners
and attest to contemporary designers' efforts to incorporate craft traditions
into works produced for modern-day Japanese society.
The designers of traditional wares have provided the commentaries
on their products and on the philosophy behind them.

18 CASIO: G-SHOCK SERIES (Model AW 500-1E, G-Mark 1988; Model BG-110-3T, G-Mark 1995; and variants)

Designer: Watch Design Department, Casio Computer Company, Ltd.

The G-Shock first appeared in 1983 as the realization of this watchmaker's simple wish to make an ultimately indestructible watch. During the first eight years, sales were concentrated mainly in the United States and only a small number were sold in Japan. In 1991, however, G-Shock watches became popular owing to the street fashions sported by young people who frequent Tokyo's Shibuya entertainment district, and Japanese sales boomed thereafter. The market is still growing, with many distinctive variants designed for the specific needs of different leisure and sports activities.

Model BG 100 OCL-7T

Model BG-110-3T

Model DW 82 00-1A

Model DW 003B-9

Model AW 500-1E

115

19 CANON: IMAGE STABILIZER BINOCULARS (G-Mark 1995)

Designer: Design Center, Canon, Inc., with Masato Hasegawa

Outdoor recreation has become very popular in Japan in recent years. Many people find birdwatching, in particular, to be an easy and relaxing way to enjoy the beauties of nature. Canon binoculars incorporate advanced technology that brings us closer to nature and helps us become better acquainted with it. Vibration-proof binoculars, which were originally developed for military use, have been redefined by Canon. This practical tool has been reduced in size and weight for the general consumer, who is promised that he or she can see even the "blinking eyes of wild birds."

20 YAMAHA: SILENT SESSION DRUM SET DTX (G-Mark 1996)

Designer: Product Design Laboratory, Yamaha Corporation

People who would like to play musical instruments in their homes are plagued by the problem of inconveniencing their neighbors, especially in Japan, where houses are small and built closely together. Sales of drum sets, which are loud and take up a considerable amount of space, have always been limited. To remedy both problems, Yamaha developed this vastly successful product. When played, it gives one the feeling of playing on actual drums. It has sound silencing features and takes up about 30 percent of the space required for a regular drum set.

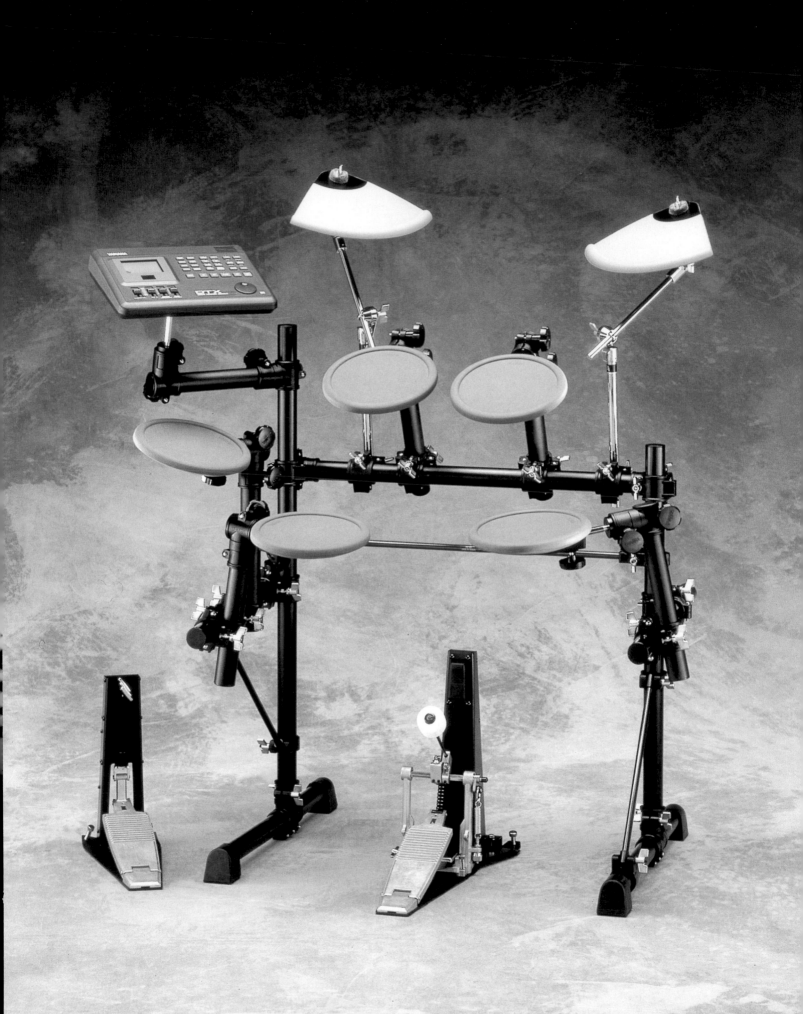

21a NTT MOBILE COMMUNICATIONS NETWORK: DIGITAL MOVA HYPER CELLULAR PHONE (G-Mark 1996 for model 101)

Designer: Toshiro Iizuka and Mikiro Ichijima of the Multimedia Life Creative Center, Matsushita Communication Industrial Company, Ltd.

21b TOSHIBA: LIBRETTO PERSONAL COMPUTER (G-Mark 1996)

Designer: Design Center, Toshiba Corporation

21c SHARP: ZAURUS PI-7000 (G-Mark 1996)

Designer: Information Systems Design Center, Sharp Corporation

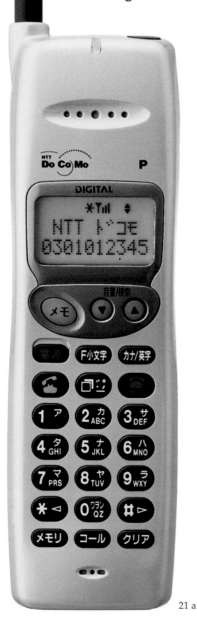

So-called PDAs (personal digital assistants), like Sharp's Zaurus, were first developed as electronic datebooks, but, with added communications functions, they can now be used in conjunction with office computers via a mobile telephone. As a result, it has become possible to do business almost anywhere, and at any time.

The Toshiba Libretto is an example of how the further miniaturization of personal computers has made them almost as mobile as PDAs. Reducing the weight and size of mobile telephones, which have been at center stage in mobile communications, remains a major technological challenge.

NTT's Do Co Mo was the first cellular phone to weigh under 100 grams, or 3.5 ounces. The success of these products indicates that mobile terminals – incorporating PDA, compact-PC, and mobile-telephone functions – will appear in the near future.

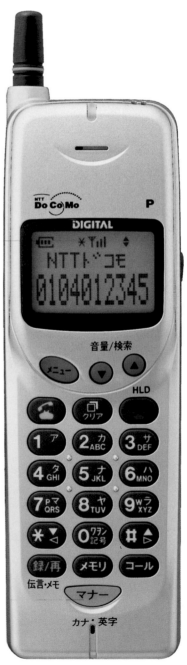

21 a

21 a

21 b

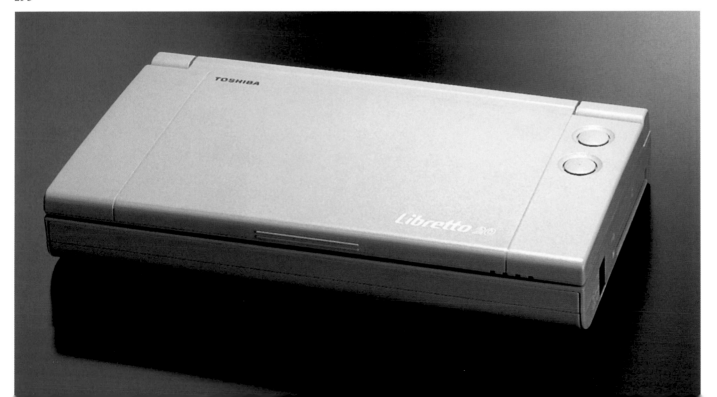

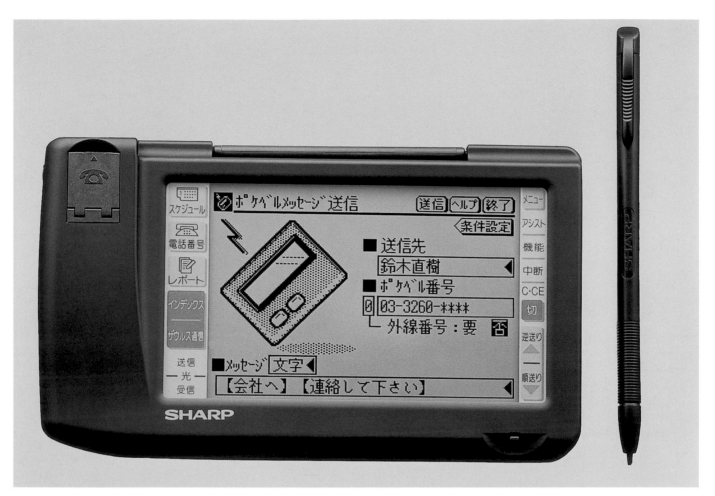

21 c

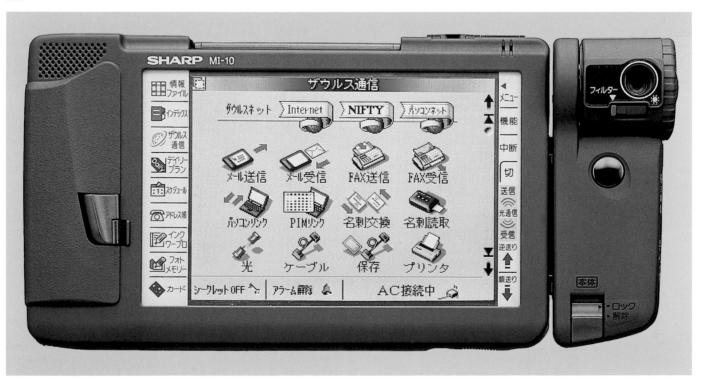

120

22a OI ELECTRIC: YOUCO PB1212 POCKET BELL (G-Mark 1995)

Designer: Engineering Division, Oi Electric Company, Ltd.

22b NTT MOBILE COMMU-NICATIONS NETWORK: SENTY NEXT G11 POCKET BELL (G-Mark 1996)

Designer: Design Center, Casio Computer Company, Ltd.

Pocket bells were first devised for business use, but, when pager functions were added, they quickly became popular among young consumers, especially as a communications device for high-school girls. This led to the emergence of a new communications subculture with its own brand of slang. Designs and colors also came to cater to what marketers felt was a young woman's predilection for "cuteness." Later, older teenagers began to use PHS (Personal Handyphone Systems), or mobile telephones, and a new trend is now developing, as elementary and junior-high-school students have begun to use pocket bells as their means of communication.

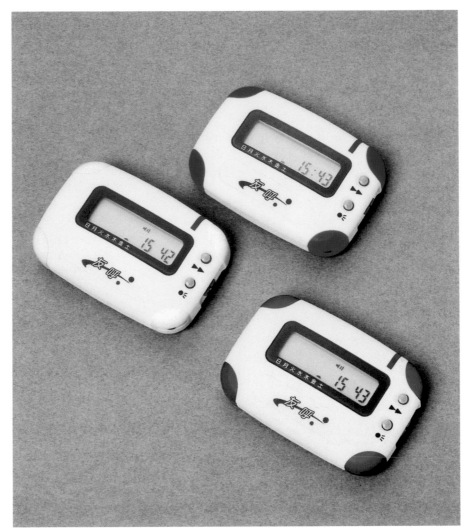

22 a

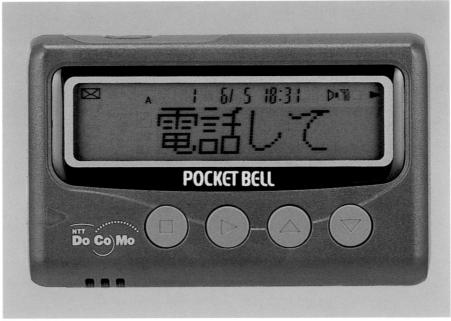

22 b

23a SONY: HANDY CAM SC55 (G-Mark 1996)

Designer: Corporate Design Center, Sony Corporation, with Mie Sakita, Assistant Designer

23b CANON: CARD-TYPE DIGITAL CAMERA CE 300 (G-Mark 1996)

Designer: Design Center, Canon, Inc., with Toru Shinano, Associate Staff Manager

In the late 1980s, Sony's Handy Cam series, based on a "passport-size" design, completely changed the image of video cameras, which had previously been large and heavy. The series was a hit with amateur users. In the early 1990s, video cameras incorporating Japan's advanced liquid-crystal technology, which made it possible to view sequences while they were being shot, became the dominant product. The Sony Handy Cam SC 55, which appeared in 1996, has a liquid-crystal display that can be set at any angle. It is one size smaller (5 ½ x 4 in.) than its predecessor, bringing it closer to design perfection. In the latter half of the 1990s, digital cameras for still photography, whose photographs could easily be "uploaded" for computer use, began to be sold. The miniature, thin Canon Digital Camera CE 300 can be plugged directly into a PC unit, where its digital images can be edited on screen.

23 a

122

23 b

24 TOTO: WASH-LET ZG/ZS (G-Mark 1996) and NEOREST EX-II (G-Mark 1993)

Designer: Industrial Design Department, TOTO, Ltd.

Japanese society prides itself on cleanliness. The Wash-Let (left) and Neorest (right), revolutionary sanitary devices that cleanse and dry the anal area, have long been successful on the Japanese market. In fact, some 30 percent of Japanese households today contain such products. The exterior has been streamlined, which entailed integrating the water spout into the toilet bowl, and a finely-calibrated water adjustment device has greatly improved the water-saving function.

25 YAMAHA: PAS (G-Mark 1994 for Model XA-1)

Designer: Yoshio Hattori, Chief Designer for Elm Design Company, Ltd., a division of the Yamaha Motor Company, Ltd.

The basic disadvantage of riding a bicycle is the strain of pedaling up hills or against the wind. The Yamaha PAS supplements the physical strength required to drive the wheels with an electric motor activated by a micro-computer. While continuing to function in the same way as a normal bicycle, it provides extra power when exertion is increased. This product is revolutionary because it has renewed the pleasures of bicycle riding for everyone, especially for the elderly.

26 HITACHI: TLAPS-1 (G-Mark 1995)

Designer: Design Center, Hitachi, Ltd., with Akitaka Takeuchi, Art Director; Toshihiko Wada, Senior Designer; and Kazuhiko Nishiyama, Designer

With the increased popularity of soccer in Japan in recent years, professional maintenance of playing fields in sports stadiums is now in high demand. To handle work that once required a great deal of labor, the Hitachi TLAPS-1 was developed as an unmanned lawn mower, applying the technology of automatic conveyor robots used in factories. In order to ensure safety, the cutting-blade is surrounded by a bumper, and sensors attached to the bumper bring the machine to a stop should it come into contact with an obstacle of any kind.

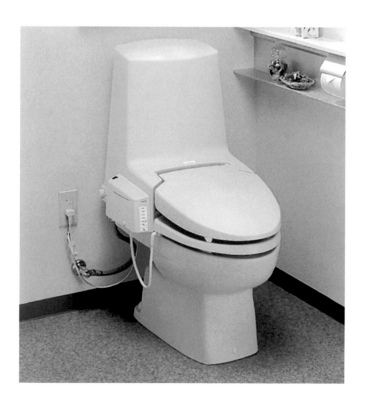

27 NTT INTELLIGENT TECHNOLOGY: MAGIC SQUARE M-301 (G-Mark 1996)

Designer: Hirano & Associates, Inc.

Magic Square employs a pattern-generating system that applies fractal-pattern technology developed by its manufacturers. Instead of repeating simple patterns of a carpet-tile type, as the previous software did, the new system makes it possible to connect several different tile patterns seamlessly, without producing unsightly design breaks. This not only helps to economize on tile-laying time and expenses, but it also makes a more artistic product, suitable for sophisticated, high-quality interiors.

28 SONY: PLAZMATRON PZ-2500 (G-Mark 1996)

Designer: Corporate Design Center, Sony Corporation, with Yuji Moriyama, Art Director

Large, flat screens are being developed to replace the deeper television tubes of today's existing technology. The Plazmatron was specially designed to be hung on the wall. Its thin display panel and innovative design with angled side speakers have given television a new image. The Plazmatron is designed for home-entertainment use and can be used in conjunction with a personal computer.

29 YAMAHA: MIBURI (G-Mark 1996)

Designer: Product Design Laboratory, Yamaha Corporation

The Miburi is a completely new medium for musical expression made possible by electronic means. Instead of the strings or keyboard common to many instruments, it takes the form of a costume equipped with sensors in various areas. The person wearing this costume "plays" the notes, controls the volume and tone quality, and sets the rhythm of the melody by moving his or her body. The development of this new genre of musical expression produced through bodily movement suggests even further horizons in the world of design.

30 XANAVI INFORMATICS: BIRD VIEW NAVIGATION SYSTEM (G-Mark 1995)

Designer: Xanavi Informatics Corporation

Car navigation systems were first installed in luxury cars in the late 1980s. Since the beginning of the 1990s, such systems have become much more affordable and now constitute a major market. Most navigation systems display maps that show the driver's position. The Bird View is the first system to display the user's location from a slightly higher elevation than his or her actual position. It has been highly praised for its presentation of navigational information "from the perspective most natural to the human senses," thereby having a direct impact on driving safety.

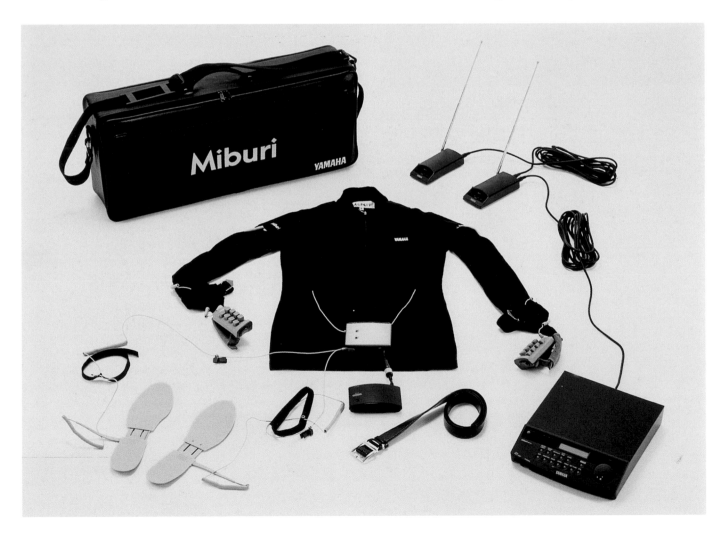

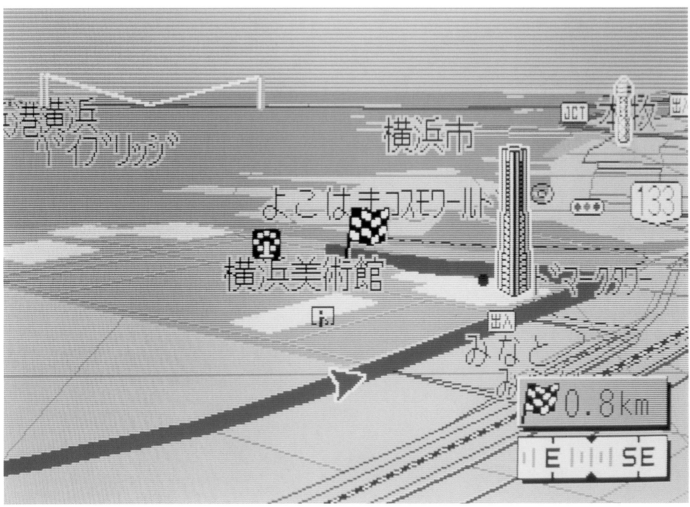

31 DAIHATSU: MIDGET II (G-Mark 1996)

Designer: Styling Division, Daihatsu Motor Company, Ltd.

Small, lightweight automobiles, which are favored by Japan's taxation system, are well suited to that country's narrow roads and tight parking conditions.

Restrictions on the maximum size of lightweight cars have been revised twice; both times the size was slightly increased. Larger size has allowed for greater comfort, yet at the expense of some of the merits of small size. The Midget II, however, is almost 17 inches shorter and 4 inches narrower than the maximum authorized size. This was accomplished by designing the car as a single-seat, pickup-style vehicle useful for traveling short distances.

32 MITSUBISHI: MINICA TOPPO (G-Mark 1993)

Designer: Office of Design, Mitsubishi Motors Corporation, with Shinichi Kobayashi, Chief Designer, and Hideki Asano, Assistant Manager

Current size restrictions on lightweight cars in Japan are approximately 10 ½ feet in length, 4½ feet in width, and 6 ½ feet in height. Only the height restriction also applies to somewhat larger compact cars. Since the beginning of the 1990s, many unique car designs optimizing this height factor have begun to appear. The Minica Toppo (signifying "high roof") features an unusual roof, which is 15 ¾ inches higher than the standard light-model body. This feature has enabled designers to redefine space in the lightweight class of mini automobile.

33 CHA LA CARTE
(Tin Teapots)

Designer: Toshiyuki Kita

The tinware made in Osaka in medieval times were once highly treasured household items. The present designs for various kinds of tea caddy and back- and side-handle teapots are attempts to bring back into people's lives the fine traditions of tin crafts in the field of "tea."

Tin is a malleable metal that can be melted at a mere 446 °F. It is also known as a material that has a purifying, flavor-enhancing effect if used to hold water or liquor, such as sake. Tin was chosen as the material for this product for these reasons and because of its capacity to be recycled. The time-honored traditional design is retained in the slip structure between the lid and body and a variety of models have been introduced, which may be used to distinguish the different types of tea inside.

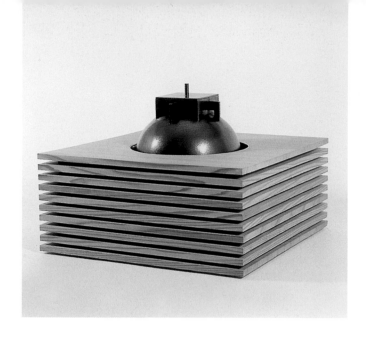
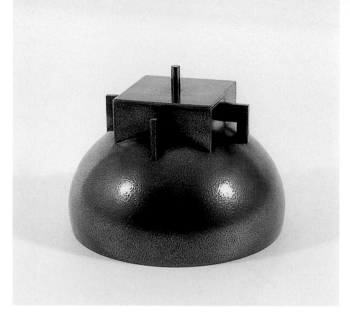

34 COPPER VESSEL SERIES FOR A JAPANESE TEA ROOM

Designer: Shigeru Uchida

Most local industries in Japan are struggling to survive. This is partly due to manufacturers' lack of understanding of contemporary life-styles. Another factor is the unnecessarily complex distribution system, in which commodities produced in regional areas are passed through the hands of a multi-layered network of profit-siphoning wholesalers and dealers before reaching consumers. This system only widens the gap between producers and consumers, preventing the former from recognizing the needs of the latter.

The demands of distribution can also lead to a decrease in the quality of the products themselves and the need to be competitive can lead to the erosion of traditional techniques. The system provides little incentive to create high-quality products or to adapt to modern society.

Many innovative local industries are attempting to do away with the wholesale network and to establish their own direct links with consumers. They have many difficulties to overcome, but the only way to achieve a genuine revival of local industry in Japan is certainly by reforming of the present distribution system.

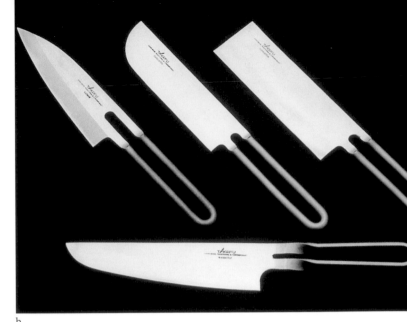

a   b

c   d

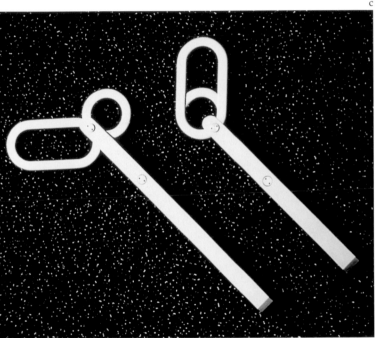
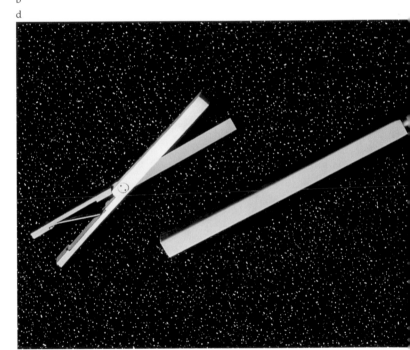

35   ECHIZEN STEEL CUTLERY
   a   **Fluctus**
   b   **Culeus**
   c   **R & R**
   d   **X & I**

Designer: Kazuo Kawasaki

Echizen cutlery draws on technology developed over the course of seven centuries by indigenous blacksmiths, who manufactured bladed implements for the farmers of Echizen Province (now Fukui Prefecture), north of Kyoto. Like many other traditional industrial arts, Echizen techniques are in danger of falling into disuse, partly because artisans have difficulty finding young craftsmen as successors and partly owing to old-fashioned production methods.

Participants in the project, which was initiated in 1983, established more efficient distribution networks and introduced modern technology and materials into the area.

Echizen knives are sold under the brand name Takefu Knife Village, and were designed to reflect international and contemporary standards of quality. These products are a striking example of innovative traditional Japanese crafts restored through modern industrial methods. It is hoped that renewed investment in other local industries will further encourage the integration of craft products into modern-day Japanese households.

36 SILVER WAVE
(Ceramic Plates)

Designer: Toshiroh Ikegami

The five thematic colors of Kutani-ware possess the warmth of the earth and the gentleness of tradition. These plates differ from the Kutani ceramics of the past in that they are made of translucent porcelain. These products are examples of high-quality goods produced in Japan today that incorporate local design techniques that have been developed over centuries.

Local industry develops in relation to such basic factors as materials, colors, texture and pattern, manufacturing methods, and distribution routes. Moreover, forms of expression change, closely reflecting the intellectual trends of the times.

In producing Silver Wave, white porcelain was used instead of ordinary clay to create the fluid, white texture. The only colors employed are the white of the porcelain and platinum silver. Projected onto the conical bowls are patterns produced by a computer-

processed photograph taken by the designer in 1991, when flying over Alaska on a flight from New York to Tokyo. In using these images of the arctic terrain to embellish the bowls, the designer has attempted to address the relationship between the earth and human beings.

37 SHIMUS WASHI PAPER ILLUMINATION

Designer: Fumio Shimizu

This project was undertaken to create the display stands for an exhibition on Japan entitled "Abitale Il Tempo" held in Verona in 1990. One of the themes of the exhibition was the utilization of locally unique resources and the use of materials through skilled handicraft techniques. For the present project, traditional Japanese washi paper was chosen as the main material.

The Verona exhibition was a valuable opportunity to show a concrete example of integrating modern design with traditional Japanese craftsmanship and materials. Personal objets d'art – implements of meditation, vases, lamps, etc. – by Japanese architects and designers were displayed on the stands. The stands were made to glow faintly in an otherwise dimly lit room, in order to make even more conspicuous the objects on display. The bases of the stands were made with cast washi, and inside them was an incandescent electric light, which illuminated the structure. The washi was produced by SHIMUS, a shop in Kyoto known for its handmade washi.

38 NEO-TSUGARU KOHIKI-DASHI (Lacquerware)

Designer: Shohei Mihara

The cultural sphere in which the sap of lacquer trees is used as a finish extends throughout East Asia. Japan's lacquer culture is perhaps the most highly developed in this area, and distinctive lacquering techniques have been passed down in various parts of the country.

Neo-Tsugaru is the application and further development of Tsugaru-Nuri techniques passed down over three hundred years in the city of Hirosaki, in Aomori Prefecture, the northernmost lacquer production area in Japan. Tsugaru-Nuri is characterized by the diversity of its patterns and motifs, which are created not by drawing but by the "shikake"

process of different treatment of several layers of colored lacquer.

Tsugaru-Nuri was designated by the Japanese government as a traditional national industrial art some decades ago, but this resulted in the establishment of a limited number of patterns. All manufacturers began producing pieces with almost the same patterns, and they were all traditional.

To move beyond these bounds, a project was launched in 1985. Headed by the Yu Studio, composed of young craftsmen, its aim was to unite the originally free spirit of Tsugaru-Nuri with modern designs and extend its applications to architectural spaces as well.

The development of new patterns was an arduous task, but nearly five hundred were created. Of these, twelve patterns judged best suited to contemporary

architectural space were singled out as being "Neo-Tsugaru." These have been favorably received.

New furniture designs and items of interior decoration using Neo-Tsugaru patterns have changed established images of lacquer products. They are now sold under the category of modern, rather than traditional, Japanese designs. The fact that they have expanded the types, and the extent, of uses to which lacquer products are put demonstrates that preserving tradition entails not only faithfully reproducing old styles but also adjusting them to the needs and tastes of the times.

39 DESK MIRROR F1-01 AND CHEST OF DRAWERS

Designer: Motomi Kawakami

This product is the result of a project undertaken in 1994-95 by three designers to create new mirror furniture for a joint venture by seven furniture manufacturers in Shizuoka in response to the Shizuoka City Local Industry Section's annual drive to encourage a revival of local industry. The traditions of Shizuoka furniture go back to lacquerware production in the Edo (1603-1867) and Meiji (1867-1911) periods. Today, Shizuoka is known for its storage furniture and particularly for dressers and other mirror-related pieces. Many small and medium-sized enterprises once flourished in this industry, but recently business has declined. There are several reasons for this. Women's life-styles and attitudes have changed considerably, yet, despite these major societal shifts, manufacturers have continued to reproduce the same established styles and ensembles. Other problems include continued reliance on outmoded wholesale systems, inadequate attempts to open up new markets, and the lack of a proper design management to oversee product development.

What is needed most is the establishment of new marketing routes and a consistent, productive collaboration between furniture-makers and designers, instead of sporadic cooperation on single projects. For this project, Kawakami produced seven designs aimed at today's women, who are increasingly pursuing their own interests and defining their own style. The design of Neo Mind Gear was based on a new concept of mirror furniture in which the traditional dressing table, associated with passivity, is replaced by a "station" at which today's more active women "recreate" themselves.

40 ARTECHNE URBAN PLUS BENCH AND ASHTRAY (Aluminum Products)

Designer: Kozo Sato

Artechne Urban Plus outdoor furniture utilizes the new "V-process" techniques for aluminum sand casting developed by Akita Light Metals Co., a leader of the local aluminum manufacturing industry for building materials in Nagano Prefecture, and is the company's first design product. Overseeing the entire production process, from the planning stage to distribution, requires a tremendous effort, and is not possible without the commitment and cooperation of the corporation's employees. Until now, the company has had no experience in the area of industrial design. Its recent activities in this field, however, are seen as an opportunity for the company to change with the times, and perhaps to create its own product development system.

New, independent manufacturing development programs, unlike made-to-order ones, are inevitably accompanied by considerable chaos in the initial stages. The design data accumulated over the approximately one year taken by this project, from the planning stage until production began, became important for developing subsequent products. One of the important results of original product development programs has been to show, using the V-process manufacturing technology, which manufacturing systems are most effective for particular shapes – something that previous made-to-order systems failed to demonstrate. The bench and ashtray introduced here are results of the former system.

As consciousness rises concerning the importance of the environment in which we live, Artechne Urban Plus outdoor furniture is a fine example of a development involving management, designers, and technicians collaborating to produce the most comfortable, attractive urban spaces possible.

41 ALUTOOL SERIES (Duralumin Tools)

Designer: Fumikazu Masuda

Alutools are produced using the special A 7001 super aluminum alloy that is used to manufacture structural parts for airplanes. For some three hundred years, the area in and around the town of Sanjō, located in the middle of Niigata Prefecture, has been known for its metal processing industry. It is among the leading areas for tool production in the country.

The Niigata Hand Tool Cooperative Association developed the Alutool series over a three-year period. This lightweight set is designed to meet the demands mainly of operators working in high places, such as high-rise buildings, and on electrical projects. The designs were based on conceptual models. The developmental stage involved commercialization, brand development, and sales promotion.

Hand tools made with dense and heavy steel are shaped for easy use and made as small as possible in order to render them as light as possible while still performing well. In using a lightweight material, such as aluminum, the designers knew they could produce high-quality products of a more flexible design.

The Alutool project began with the selection of materials and the development of processing methods, while overcoming technical problems through various innovative solutions, such as using steel or stainless steel for specific parts of the tools. The pace of development varied, because each item was produced by a different company. Consistency of design was maintained by means of flexible guidelines regarding the individual features of the companies involved.

Aluminum refining consumes large amounts of electricity; however, 99 percent of it can be recycled, which requires only $1/36$th of the original amount of energy. One of the themes of the Alutool series was its capacity to be recycled. Toward that end, almost all the non-aluminum components are designed for easy separation.

42 CHAOS (Wristwatch)

Designer: Masayuki Kurokawa

This dual watch in a titanium frame displays a small window in the main clock face, which indicates whether it is daytime or nighttime. The design is emblematic of the new age: unisex fashion, internationalism, a concern for materials, and the "wild" look.

What is unique about this product is that it was manufactured by a large corporation, designed by a single independent designer in collaboration with a small enterprise specializing mainly in traditional crafts, and marketed by all three. Hence, the paradigm of Japanese business that has prevailed until now, in which small businesses were invariably subcontracted to work for larger ones, is in the process of changing.

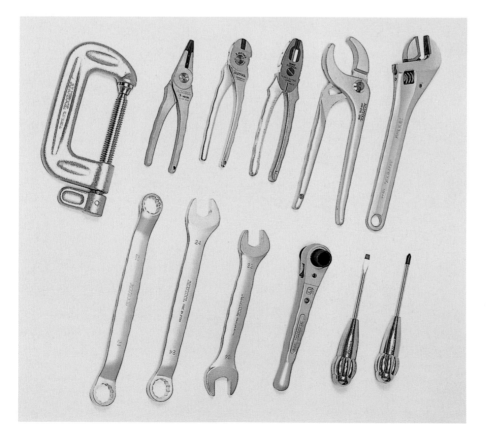

APPENDIX

BIOGRAPHICAL GLOSSARY

Architects

Hitoshi Abe

Hitoshi Abe was born in Sendai, Miyagi Prefecture, in 1962. He received his master's degree in architecture in 1989 from the Southern California Institute of Architecture. From 1988 to 1992, he worked for Coop Himmelblau in Los Angeles. In 1992, he received his doctorate in architecture from Tōhoku University and established Atelier Hitoshi Abe in Sendai. His completed works include the Miyagi Water Tower (1994) and Shirasagi Bridge (1994). In 1997, he received the World Architecture Award at the World Triennale of Architecture INTER ARCH '97 in Sofia, Bulgaria.

Jun Aoki

Born in 1956 in Yokohama, Jun Aoki received his bachelor's degree in architecture from the University

of Tokyo and subsequently took up a position, which he held from 1983 to 1990, at Arata Isozaki & Associates. In 1991, he established his own architectural firm. He has designed numerous houses in and around Tokyo and his recently completed Yusuikan swimming pool (1997) is in Toyosaka. He is currently overseeing public proj-

ects, such as a museum in Niigata Prefecture and a primary school in Nara Prefecture.

Coelacanth Architects, Inc.

In 1985, a group of architects began cooperating professionally under the name of Coelacanth Architects. In 1986, the firm of Coelacanth Architects, Inc. was founded by Yasuyuki Ito, Kazumi Kudo, Masao Koizumi, Kazuhiro Kojima, Hiroshi Horiba, and Maho Hiiro. Currently, it is composed of eight partners, including Mitsumasa Sanpei and Susumu Uno. The firm's major works include the Sakuradai Apartment House, Tokyo (1990); the Osaka International Peace Center, Osaka (1991); and the Chiba Municipal Utase Elementary School, Chiba (1995). The architects have received several awards for their work, among them the Prize of the Architectural Institute of Japan for Design in 1997.

Norihiko Dan

Born in 1956 in Hayama Town, Kanagawa Prefecture, Norihiko Dan earned his bachelor's degree in architecture from the University of Tokyo in 1979 and his master's degree from the same institution in 1982. Within two years, he had received another masters's degree in architecture from Yale University and, in 1986, he founded the firm Dan & Aoshima Associates. In 1995, he established Norihiko Dan and Associates. His works have been published internationally. Recent examples include the Minami Ohsawa police box in the Hachiōji district of Tokyo (1993) and the Kyū-Karuizawa Clubhouse (1996).

Hiroshi Hara

Hiroshi Hara

Born in 1936 in Kawasaki City, Hiroshi Hara studied architecture at the University of Tokyo, receiving his bachelor's degree in 1959, his master's in 1961, and his doctorate in 1964, at which time he joined the faculty of his alma mater's Department of Architecture. In 1970, he founded Atelier Φ. His major works include the Josei Primary School in Okinawa's Naha City (1987), the Tokyo headquarters for Yamato International (1986), and Osaka's Umeda Sky Building (1993). He is currently working on a number of public projects, including his competition-winning design for the reconstruction of the JR Kyoto Station and a new high school in Hiroshima, which will be built in conjunction with the city's P+C Building Program.

Shoichi Haryu

Born in 1942 in Natori, Miyagi Prefecture, Shoichi Haryu graduated from Tōhku University in 1968 with a master's degree in engineering. In 1968, he began working at Daiichi-Kobo Associates

and remained there until 1981, when he opened his own office, Shoichi Haryu Architect & Associates, in Sendai. His completed works include the Sendai Arinomamasya Welfare Home for the Aged (1987), the Marumori Sairi Yashiki Museum (1988), and the Natori City Crematorium (1995). He is currently working on several other public projects in Miyagi Prefecture, such as additions to the Sendai Yagiyama Zoo and the Shichigahama Stadium and Sports Arena.

Haryu & Abe Cooperative Atelier

In 1992, Shoichi Haryu and Hitoshi Abe took First Prize in the open competition for Miyagi Stadium. In 1993, they established Haryu & Abe Cooperative Atelier to collaborate on the stadium.

Itsuko Hasegawa

Itsuko Hasegawa was born in Yaizu City, Shizuoka Prefecture, in 1941. After graduating from the Department of Architecture at Kanto Gakuin University, Itsuko Hasegawa became a research student in the Department of Architecture at the Tokyo Institute of Technology. In 1979, she established the Itsuko Hasegawa Atelier. Her projects include a variety of houses and public buildings. In 1986, she received the Prize of the Architectural Institute of Japan for Design for Bizan Hall, a multipurpose space for students and faculty alike, located in the private university of Shizuoka Seika Gakuen, Shizuoka City. Her residential projects also earned her the Japan Cultural Design Award in 1986. That same year, she won the competition for the Shonandai Cultural Center, which was completed in 1990.

Arata Isozaki

Born in 1931 in Ōita City, Arata Isozaki graduated in 1954 from the University of Tokyo with a degree in architecture and, in 1963, he established his current firm, Arata Isozaki & Associates. He has won numerous international awards, among them the Gold Medal of the Royal Institute of British Architects in 1986. His major buildings are scattered across the globe and include the Museum of Contemporary Art in Los Angeles (1981-86), the Palau D'Esports Sant Jordi in Barcelona (1983-90), the Team Disney Building in Orlando (1987-90), and the Center for Japanese Art and Technology in Kraków (1990-94).

Toyo Ito

Born in 1941 in Seoul, Korea, Toyo Ito studied architecture at the University of Tokyo, where he graduated in 1965. For the next few years he worked for Kiyonori Kikutake Architect and Associates until he established his own practice in 1971. In 1979, he renamed his firm Toyo Ito & Associates, Architects. He has exhibited, published, and built internationally, receiving numerous awards. Recent works include the Eckenheim Municipal Kindergarten (1993) in Frankfurt am Main, the Fire Station in Yatsushiro, Kumamato Prefecture (1995), and an installation in the exhibition "Japan Today '95: The Third Reality," held in 1995 in the Louisiana Museum, Humlebeak, outside Copenhagen.

Hideaki Katsura

Hideaki Katsura was born in 1952 in Kitakyūshū City, Fukuoka Prefecture. In 1979, he completed

his graduate course in architecture at Kumamoto University. In 1990, he formed a partnership with A.I.R. His completed works include the Yunomae Cartoon Museum and Community Center (1992), which is a Kumamoto Artpolis project, and the Kyusendo Bio-Center (1994), also in Kumamoto Prefecture. His work has been published extensively in Japan.

Kengo Kuma

Born in 1954 in Kanagawa Prefecture, Kengo Kuma graduated from the University of Tokyo with a master's degree in architecture in 1979. Before and after establishing his current firm in 1990, he worked independently, received fellowships and lectureships, and exhibited and published his work internationally. His recent works include the Club House for the Kinojo Golf Club in Okayama (1992), the "Water/Glass" Guest House in Shizuoka (1995), and the design of the Japanese Pavilion for the Venice Biennale (1995).

Kisho Kurokawa

Born in Nagoya in 1934, Kisho Kurokawa studied at Kyoto University, and graduated with a bachelor's degree in architecture in 1957. He earned his master's degree in architecture in 1959 and his doctorate in architecture in 1964, both from the University of Tokyo. At the age of twenty-five, he became one of the founders of the Metabolism Movement. Since then he has written many books on architecture and has designed numerous award-winning buildings. For his architectural achievements, Kurokawa has received the Gold Medal from the French Academy of Architecture and the Chevalier de l'Ordre des Arts et des Lettres from the French

Minister of Culture. In Japan, he has received, among others, the Takamura Kotaro Design Award, the Mainichi Art Award, the Prize of the Architectural Institute of Japan for Design, and the highest prize from the Japan Art Academy. His major buildings include the National Museum of Ethnology in Osaka (1977), the Nara City Museum of Photography (1991), the Museum of Modern Art Wakayama/Wakayama Prefectural Museum (1994), and the Ehime Prefectural Museum of General Science (1994). One of his latest works is the new KL International Airport at Kuala Lumpur (1994-97, first phase).

Fumihiko Maki

Born in Tokyo in 1928, Fumihiko Maki earned his bachelor's degree in architecture in 1952 from the University of Tokyo, a master's degree in architecture in 1953 from the Cranbrook Academy of Art in Bloomfield Hills, Michigan, and a master's degree in architecture from Harvard University's Graduate School of Design in 1954. In addition to an active architec-

tural and teaching career, he has received numerous prestigious awards, including the Pritzker Architecture Prize (1993), the Gold Medal of the Union of International Architects (1993), and the Prince of Wales' Prize in Urban Design (1993). He has designed buildings in Japan, Europe, and the United States. His most recent works include the Tokyo Metropolitan Gymnasium (1990), the Isar Büropark outside Munich (1995), the Center for the Arts in Yerba Buena Gardens, San Francisco (1993), and the Tokyo Church of Christ (1995).

Hiroshi Naito

Born in Yokohama in 1950, Hiroshi Naito graduated from Waseda University in Tokyo in 1974 and attended the graduate school there from 1974 to 1976. After working with architects in Madrid and Tokyo, he established his own office in 1981, designing works such as the Gallery TOM in Tokyo (1984), the Sea Folk Museum in Toba City, Mie Prefecture (1992), and the Shima Art Museum (1993). His Ushibuka Fisherman's Wharf, which was commissioned as part of Kumamoto's Artpolis program, was completed in 1997.

Kazuyo Sejima

Born in 1958 in Hitachi City, Ibaraki Prefecture, Kazuyo Sejima graduated from Japan Women's University with a master's degree in architecture in 1981. In 1987, she established Kazuyo Sejima & Associates. In addition to lecturing on architecture at various Japanese universities and exhibiting in a number of shows, she has designed and built a variety of houses and other buildings, ranging from the Castelbajac Sports Shop in Yokohama City (1991) to three Pachinko Parlors (1993, 1996) and the neighborhood police box at Tokyo's Chōfu Station (1995).

Teiichi Takahashi

Teiichi Takahashi was born in Tsingtao (otherwise known as Qingdao), China, in 1924. After graduating from the University of Tokyo in 1949, he started working for the government in the architectural division of the Ministry of Posts and Telecommunications. Seven years later, he was appointed assistant professor of architecture at the Musashi Institute of Technology. In 1963, he resigned from the school after

winning a competition for the campus of the Osaka University of Arts. That same year, he established a small atelier called Daiichi-Kobo Associates with three colleagues. The name Daiichi-Kobo (which means "The Premier Atelier") was chosen instead of naming the firm after one architect. His most recent completed works include the Tokyo Metropolitan University (1991), the Toyo University Hakusan Campus, Tokyo (1994), and the Zenrosai Computer Center, Tokyo (1995). Presently his office consists of five partners and twenty-five staff members.

Yoshio Taniguchi

Yoshio Taniguchi was born in Tokyo in 1937. In 1960, he received a bachelor's degree in mechanical engineering from Tokyo's Keio University and, in 1964, he received his master's degree in architecture from Harvard University's Grad-

uate School of Design. From 1964 through 1972, he worked with Kenzo Tange in various capacities. In 1975, he established his own practice. He has undertaken numerous public design commissions for museums, libraries, and schools. His completed works include the Tokyo Sealife Park (1989), Keio Shonan-Fujisawa Junior and Senior High School (1992), and the Toyota Municipal Museum of Art (1995). He has taught at universities, both at home and abroad, and, in 1996, he was appointed Honorary Fellow by the American Institute of Architects.

Riken Yamamoto

Riken Yamamoto was born in 1945 in Beijing. After graduating from the school of architecture at Nihon University in 1968, he completed

his master's degree in architecture at the University of Tokyo in 1971 and worked under Hiroshi Hara at the University's Institute of Industrial Science from 1971 to 1973, after which he established the firm Riken Yamamoto & Field Shop. Since then, he has won awards at home and abroad for various projects. His recent works include Hotakubo Housing, Kumamoto City (1991), built for Kumamoto Prefecture's Artpolis program, and the multi-purpose buildings at Ryokuen-Toshi (Interjunction City; 1992-94). He is currently working on a number of public projects, such as the Hiroshima Nishi Fire Station and the Hakodate Municipal College, both competition-winning designs.

Designers

Toshiroh Ikegami

Born in Osaka in 1948, Toshiro Ikegami earned his bachelor's degree in architecture from Osaka University in 1974, working briefly thereafter in a city planning office called the Urban Planning Institute as well as in Tadao Ando's architectural firm in 1976. He established his own architectural practice in 1981, and works in a variety of design fields besides architecture. His projects have won awards, including the Gold Prize of the Japan Design Foundation in 1983 for his Public Chair Prototype, and the Second Prize Interior Design Award in 1994 for a Dwelling in Hiro, Tokyo, as well as an Honorable Mention, in 1995, from the Japan Federation of Architects & Building Engineers Association.

Motomi Kawakami

Born in 1940 in Hyōgo Prefecture, Motomi Kawakami graduated in 1964 from the Tokyo National University of Fine Arts and Music, where he studied industrial design.

Motomi Kawakami

After engaging in postgraduate work in art at the same institution for two years, he went to Milan to work with the architect Angelo Mangiarotti from 1966 to 1969. In 1971, after returning to Japan, he established his own design office, which specializes in interior, product, and environmental design. He also teaches at various Japanese design schools. His work has been extensively exhibited, and he has received awards, such as the Yokohama Civic Design Award (1996), the Kitaro Kuni Industrial Design Award (1992), the Japan Package Design Award for Excellence (1985, 1986), and the Japan Interior Design Award for Excellence (1984).

Kazuo Kawasaki

Born in 1949 in Fukui City, Kazuo Kawasaki graduated in 1972 from the Kanazawa College of Art, where he studied industrial design. Immediately thereafter, he took up a post with Toshiba, where he designed hi-fi equipment. In 1979, he established his own design studio and, in 1985, he founded eX-DESIGN INC,

which advises Apple, and designs a variety of products, from traditional crafts to computer systems. It also advises in the fields of corporate strategy and regional business planning. Kawasaki has won numerous awards, including the German International Design Award (1993), and is currently Professor at the School of Design and Architecture at Nagoya City University.

Toshiyuki Kita

Born in 1942 in Osaka, Toshiyuki Kita graduated in 1964 from Naniwa College in Osaka, where

he studied industrial design. After a brief sojourn in Milan, he returned to Japan, where he now practices environmental, interior, and product design. His works are in museum collections, including The Museum of Modern Art in New York. Among his more recent projects are the seating and interior of the rotating theater in the Japanese Pavilion at the 1992 World's Fair in Seville. He has also received such design awards as the Product Design Awards from the Institute of Business Designers in the United States (1983) and the Delta de Oro in Spain (1990).

Masayuki Kurokawa

Born 1937 in Aichi Prefecture, Masayuki Kurokawa attended the Nagoya Institute of Technology, where he studied architecture, graduating in 1961. Like his older brother Kisho Kurokawa, he earned a doctorate in architecture – in his case, from Waseda University in 1967. Masayuki Kurokawa established his own architectural firm shortly thereafter. He has designed a number of products

found in the permanent collection of The Museum of Modern Art in New York. He received the Mainichi Design Award in 1985, and has been a Professor in the Graduate School of Art at Nihon University since 1993. His work was the subject of a monograph published that year by Rikuyo-sya Press.

Fumikazu Masuda

Born in Tokyo in 1949, Fumikazu Masuda graduated from Tokyo University of Art and Design with a bachelor's degree in design in 1973. He has practiced as an industrial designer of products and consumer goods from 1978 onward. Since 1991, when he established his current design firm Open House, he has begun to work with small, local companies. At the same time, he has become involved in ecological design, and has organized an international workshop and several exhibitions on this subject, while working to discover and develop new materials for environmentally friendly products.

Fumikazu Masuda

Shohei Mihara

Born in 1947 in Fukushima Prefecture, Shohei Mihara graduated from Tokyo University of Art and Design in 1970 and three years later he cofounded the P&P Design Research Center. In 1985, he formed the Radical Design Studio, renaming it Shohei Mihara Design Studio in 1993. His recent efforts include an exhibition of his works in "Today's Japan Design Sampling '95," Toronto, 1995, and, in 1997, the founding of *Web Design* magazine.

Kozo Sato

Born in Tokyo in 1951, Kozo Sato attended the Design Polytechnic in Milan from 1973 to 1976, where

Kozo Sato

he graduated from the Department of Industrial Design. After working for the Rodolfo Bonetto Studio from 1976 to 1980, he returned to Tokyo to establish the Kozo Design Studio in 1983. With product design as his main focus, he also engages in a variety of design disciplines from environmental design to museum planning. His products received G-Mark awards in 1988, 1991, and 1993, and his works are in the permanent collections of the Cooper Hewitt Museum in New York and the Musée des arts décoratifs in Montreal. In addition to designing, he teaches at the Tama Art University.

Fumio Shimizu

Born in Shimane in 1950, Fumio Shimizu attended and graduated from various schools, including the Shibaura Institute of Technology in Tokyo, the Architectural Association in London, and the Polytechnic in Milan. In 1988, he founded his own architectural firm in Tokyo, specializing in architecture as well as interior and industrial design. He has been a curator of various design

exhibitions as well as a participant in such shows, and acted as the director of *FP* magazine from 1989 to 1993, the editor of *KUKAN* magazine from 1990 to 1992, and the editor-in-chief of *JAPAN AVENUE* magazine in 1993-94. He teaches design at the Kanto Gakuin University, the Tokyo Technical College, and the Shibaura Institute of Technology.

Shigeru Uchida

Born in Yokohama in 1943, Shigeru Uchida graduated from the Kuwasawa Design School in 1966 and established his own practice in 1970. His current firm, Studio 80, was established in 1981. He has designed a number of boutiques for Issey Miyake and Yohji Yamamoto as well as the Hotel Il Palazzo in Fukuoka and the Kobe Fashion Museum. His tea room products and furniture are sold throughout the world and are represented in a variety of museum collections, as well as having been extensively published internationally.

CONTRIBUTORS

John Heskett

studied at the London School of Economics from 1957 to 1960. He is Professor of Design at the Institute of Design, Illinois Institute of Technology in Chicago, where he teaches design theory and history. He is the author of *Industrial Design* (1980), widely used as a basic textbook for design courses in many countries, and subsequently published *Design in Germany, 1870–1918* (1986) and *Philips: A Study of the Corporate Management of Design* (1989). His current research includes a study of government design policy in countries around the world. In addition to writing and lecturing internationally on design, he has acted as a consultant to governmental bodies and educational organizations in many countries. He is an Executive Consultant for the Hirano Design Group, a major Japanese consultancy with offices in Tokyo and Chicago, and is Visiting Professor at Tama Art University in Tokyo.

Takuo Hirano

graduated from the Technical Art Course of the School of Art at the Tokyo National University of Fine Arts and Music in 1953. In 1955, he left Japan to study in the United States under the auspices of a government-sponsored program. Upon returning to Japan he proposed the establishment of "The Good Design Products Selection System" to promote greater awareness of design in Japan. He is currently the chairman of the Tokyo-based industrial and architectural design firm, Hirano Design Sekkei, and serves on various committees of the Ministry for International Trade and Industry. His achievements in promoting international exchange and culture in regional areas through design are numerous. He is also a trustee and a Professor at Tama Art University and has taught at several universities in Japan.

Tadanori Nagasawa

graduated from the College of Art and Design at the Musashino Art University in Tokyo in 1978. He is a design consultant, designer, cultural engineer, and the President of Tadanori Nagasawa & Associates, Limited, and Associate Professor at the Tōhoku University of Art and Design. He is well known in Japan as a leading design impresario and policymaker. He advises the national government and several regional authorities, as well as professional associations and private-sector clients, on all aspects of design policy. He has been a member of the juries of many design competitions and has been invited to chair, or speak at, many design seminars throughout Japan, and has also organized a variety of local and national design conventions, exhibitions, and conferences. He is the author of numerous magazine articles and design books, including a 1988 volume entitled *The Intangible Era.*

Naomi R. Pollock

is an American architect living in Tokyo, where she writes about architecture and design. Her work has appeared in publications on both sides of the Pacific, including *Inland Architect, Interior Design, Metropolis, Monthly Korean Architects, The New York Times,* and *Architectural Record,* for whom she has been a correspondent since 1990. She received a master's degree in architecture from Harvard University's Graduate School of Design in 1985 and a master's degree in engineering from the Department of Architecture at Tokyo University in 1991.

Hiroyuki Suzuki

is Professor of Architectural History at Tokyo University. He received his Ph.D. from Tokyo University in 1984. He has taught and lectured at many universities both in Japan and abroad. He is

155

the author of a number of books in English and in Japanese, including *Contemporary Architecture of Japan: 1958–1984* and *100 Western Style Buildings in the Meiji Era*. As a translator of architectural texts, Suzuki has made accessible to a Japanese-speaking audience such English-language works as *Classical Language of Architecture* by Sir John Summerson, *Ruskin and Viollet-le-Duc* by Sir Nicholas Pevsner, and *The History of Architecture* by Spiro Kostof. In addition, Suzuki has written numerous articles in English about Japanese architecture, which have appeared in a variety of publications in Japan and in the West.

John Zukowsky

received his Ph. D. from the State University of New York at Binghampton. As Curator of Architecture at The Art Institute of Chicago, he has organized numerous exhibitions and has edited numerous publications, some of which deal with both architecture and industrial design, such as *Austrian Architecture and Design: Beyond Tradition in the 1990s* (1991) and, most recently, *Building for Air Travel: Architecture and Design for Commercial Aviation* (1996), which further investigates the interdependent relationship between both disciplines.

INDEX

Numbers in *italics* refer to pages with illustrations.

Abe, Hitoshi *44, 45, 47,* 56
Ando, Tadao 15
Aoki, Jun 36, *36,* 50
Aoki, Ryuya *111*
Asada, Takashi 23
Asano, Hideki 130

Banham, Reyner 33

Canon, Inc., Design Center 116, 122
Casio Computer Company, Ltd., Design Center 121
Casio Computer Company, Ltd., Watch Design Department 114
Coelacanth Architects, Inc. 52

Daihatsu Motor Company, Ltd., Styling Division 130
Dan, Norihiko 40, 42, 43, *43,* 53

Ekuan, Kenji 85
Elm Design Company, Ltd. (a division of Yamaha Motor Company, Ltd.) 124

Hara, Hiroshi 54
Haryu, Shoichi (Haryu & Abe Cooperative Atelier) *44,* 56
Hasegawa, Itsuko 39, *40,* 44, 45, 55
Hasegawa, Masato 116
Hattori, Yoshio 124
Herron, Ron, Associates *37*
Hirakura, Naoko, Associates *30, 38*
Hirano, Takuo (Hirano & Associates) 85, 92, 126
Hitachi, Ltd., Design Center 124

Ichijima, Mikiro 118
Iizuka, Toshiro 118

Igarashi, Takenobu *102*
Ikegami, Toshiroh 136
Isozaki, Arata 15, 25, 28, *28,* 32, 35, 36, 39, 58, 72
Ito, Toyo 15, 45, *45,* 60

Kamo, Kiwako *37*
Kamoshida, Atsuko 84
Katsura, Hideaki 61
Kawakami, Motomi 139
Kawasaki, Kazuo 135
Kita, Toshiyuki 132
Kobayashi, Shinichi 130
Kuma, Kengo 40, *41,* 64
Kuramori & Associates 58
Kurokawa, Kisho 15, 28, *29,* 66
Kurokawa, Masayuki 95, 142

Maekawa, Kunio 25
Maki, Fumihiko 15, 34, 41, 42, 69
Masuda, Fumikazu 142
Matsushita Communication Industrial Company, Ltd., Multimedia Life Creative Center *103,* 118
Mies van der Rohe, Ludwig 27
Mihara, Shohei 138
Mitani, Toru 41
Mitsubishi Motors Corporation, Office of Design 130
Moriyama, Yuji 126
Murano, Togo 21-23, *20, 24*

Naito, Hiroshi 68
Nishiyama, Kazuhiko 124
Nishizawa, Ryue 72

Oi Electric Company, Ltd., Engineering Division 121
Okada, Hiroyuki *110*
Okada, Shinichi 37
Otani, Sachio 23

Sakai, Naoki 92
Sakita, Mie 122
Sato, Kozo 141
Sato, Takeo 25
Sejima, Kazuyo 72
Sekkei, Nikken 17
Sharp Corporation, Information Systems Design Center 118
Shimizu, Fumio 137
Shinano, Toru 122
Shirai, Seiichi 25
Sony Corporation, Corporate Design Center 122, 126
Starck, Philippe *34*
Suzuki, Hiroyuki 33, 41, 46

Takahashi, Teiichi 73
Takenaga, Keiichi *111*
Takeuchi, Akitaka 124
Tange, Kenzo 15, *16,* 21-23, *22, 24, 28,* 33
Taniguchi, Yoshio 46, *46,* 76
Tardits, Manuel *37*
Toshiba Corporation, Design Center 118
TOTO, Ltd., Industrial Design Department 124

Uchida, Shigeru 134
Uchida, Yoshikazu 25

Wada, Toshihiko 124

Xanavi Informatics Corporation 128

Yamaha Corporation, Product Design Laboratory 116, 128
Yamaha Motor Company, Ltd. 124
Yamamoto, Riken 38, 39, *39,* 78
Yatsuka, Hajime 35

PHOTOGRAPHY CREDITS

Photographs were provided by the respective authors, architects, designers, or manufacturers. Individual acknowledgments are as follows:

Pollock

4: Jun Aoki
8, 10: Mitsumasa Fujitsuka, Helico Company, Ltd.
9: Kenichi Suzuki, © Shinken-chiku-sha Co., Ltd.
11, 12: © Shinkenchiku-sha Co., Ltd.
13: Hitoshi Abe
14: © Tomio Ohashi
15: Yoshio Taniguchi

Architecture Plates

1, 14: Hiroshi Ueda, © GA Photographers

3   (p. 53, top), 9 (pp. 61, 62-63, double-page spread): © Shinkenchiku-sha Co., Ltd.
6: computer drawings by Masaaki Onuma
7, 10, 17 (p. 79, top): Mitsumasa Fujitsuka, Helico Company, Ltd.
8: © Tomio Ohashi
11: Yuji Takeuchi, © S. S. Hokuriku
13: Toshiharu Kitajima, Archi-Photo
15: pp. 73, 74 (top right and bottom), 75 (bottom) Katsuhisa Kida

Nagasawa

1: © Umezu Takayuki, Courtesy of Yajima Shinji
2-5: © Japan Industrial Design Promotion Organization
6-8, 10-12: © Industrial Technology Research Institute of Saitama,

Courtesy of Kageyama Kazunori
9: © Umezu Takayuki

Biographical Glossary

Abe: Eiji Kitada
Coelacanth Architects, Inc.: © Nacása & Partners inc.
Haryu: Eiji Kitada
Isozaki: © Eiichiro Sakata
Naito: © Nacása & Partners inc.
Takahashi: Katsuhisa Kida
Yamamoto: © Tadashi Wakui